Grace Abounding

Grace Abounding

Georgia Harkness

Abingdon Press
Nashville and New York

To
VERNA
who shares my home and my life
and to whom the book and its author owe much

CONTENTS

Introduction   11

I. Deep Rootage
1. *Stump Fence*   19
2. *Blessedness*   23
3. *Eucharist*   27
4. *God of the Fertile Fields* 30
5. *Benediction*   34
6. *School Days*   38
7. *Permanence*   41

II. God Speaks Through His World
8. *Dayspring*   47
9. *The Strength of the Hills Is His Also*   50
10. *God's Clarion*   53
11. *Cloth of Gold*   56
12. *My Lake*   59
13. *Sounds*   62
14. *Fairyland and Cathedrals* 65
15. *Hymn to the Sun*   68
16. *Moonlight*   71
17. *Miracle*   74

III.   Great Days of Our Faith

    18.   *Christmas*   79

    19.   *Good Friday*   82

    20.   *Easter Joy*   85

    21.   *Easter Mandate*   88

    22.   *How Do I Know?*   92

    23.   *Pentecost*   94

    24.   *Thanksgiving*   98

IV.   They Live Again

    25.   *Eternal Tribute*   103

    26.   *To One Who Spent*

         Herself Early   105

    27.   *Postlude*   109

    28.   *The Upward Path*   112

    29.   *To a Gentle Soul of*

         Valiant Strength   115

    30.   *To a Christian Saint*   118

V.   In Quest of a Better Society

    31.   *Holy Flame*   125

    32.   *The Treaty*   128

    33.   *The Innocents*   133

    34.   *For Conscience*   136

    35.   *Black*   139

    36.   *Walls*   142

    37   *The Carolers*   145

    38.   *Shall I Crucify?*   148

    39.   *The Earth Thou Gavest* 152

    40.   *Forward!*   155

VI. Variant Moods
    41. *Fruitage*   161
    42. *Accidie*   164
    43. *Wet Grass*   167
    44. *The Quest*   169
    45. *Rest in the Lord*   173
    46. *Hilltop at Morning*   176
    47. *This Ministry*   179
    48. *The Divine Patience*   182
    49. *The Maker*   186
    50. *Transiency*   189

INTRODUCTION

Almost exactly three centuries ago an English tinker and thinker, John Bunyan, wrote a book entitled *Grace Abounding to the Chief of Sinners.* Like his more famous *Pilgrim's Progress,* it was written when he was in jail for conscience's sake for preaching in defiance of the law. Unlike *Pilgrim's Progress* it did not become a classic piece of writing. It is Bunyan's spiritual autobiography. It has some moving passages, but most modern readers would find its style archaic.

Whatever its interest or value today, *Grace Abounding*—for it is by this designation that the book is generally known—has a wonderful title. It ought not to be preempted for all time by a book written three hundred years ago and now seldom looked into. Accordingly, I have shamelessly appropriated the title, though I prefer to leave it with the Lord as to who may be the chief of sinners. If the soul of John Bunyan from the Celestial City objects to this plagiarism, I apologize; at least, I give credit to my source. If it is true that "imitation is the sincerest flattery," he might be pleased.

The primary purpose of this little volume of mine is to witness to the abounding grace of God in

11

human living and throughout God's world. These are times of deep anxiety, of unrest, of spreading violence, of distrust of many of our institutions—including the church. Old moorings have broken loose, and in spite of some signs of progress in human affairs there is a widespread sense of futility, estrangement, and malaise abroad in the land.

How is this state of affairs to be met? Clearly, by a better ordering of social relations in matters of family life, race, politics, economics, the preservation of an orderly and responsible society. But this is not all. We shall not have the kind of reconstructed society for which thoughtful persons long and many labor without a recovery of the inner fabric of its people's lives. We need desperately an inner confidence and a sense of life's meaning—a conviction that in spite of the pain and evil all too evident, this is still at base a good and meaningful world.

There are many ways to say this, and it is often said. The Christian way is to say that we need confidence in a divine control of our world and the faith that human effort is meaningful to the degree that it is aligned with the long purposes of God. In short, the times call for trust in the goodness of God and gratitude for God's unfailing and abounding grace.

If this book contributes even a little to such a renewed confidence and trust, it will have fulfilled its primary purpose. Yet it has three subpurposes, which I hope may contribute to rather than deflect from its primary one.

One of these is to bring together some of my unpublished and no longer extant poems. Since the 1930's when I first discovered the pleasures of writing verse, my publishers have issued two devotional manuals consisting of poems and prayers, *The Glory of God* in 1943 and *Be Still and Know* in 1953. My earliest book of verse, *Holy Flame,* first published in 1935, has now been out of print for nearly twenty years. With a very few exceptions the present volume contains only poems previously unpublished or those which have appeared only in *Holy Flame* and so are no longer available.

A second subpurpose is to make the poems more meaningful by saying something of the circumstances which prompted the writing of them. This is not that I wish to explain them, for any poem worthy of publication at all ought to convey its own meaning, however subtly stated. (The reader will soon discern that I do not go along with much of the unstructured and near-meaningless prose which is in vogue as poetry today!) Nevertheless, since every poem is written because of some particular occasion or circumstance, why not let the reader know what called it forth?

About a third subpurpose I have more hesitancy. Whether it blends successfully with these other goals the reader must decide. This subpurpose is to present something of my own spiritual autobiography.

It has more than once been suggested to me that I ought to write my life story, for regardless of having written a considerable number of books, it is a bit unusual for a woman to have served as a professor of Christian theology for twenty-two years in two major seminaries. This suggestion I have resisted, first, for lack of anything so unusual about my life as to make it of interest to others and, second, because of the difficulty in writing an autobiography that is not egocentric. Dr. Fosdick said it for me some years before his book *The Living of These Days* appeared. When asked why he did not write his own life story, he replied, "How can you write an autobiography without talking about yourself?" Yet later he did it, to the profit of all readers.

For these reasons I do not plan to write a full-length personal history. Yet there are things in my background and years of experience that are a witness to the encompassing and abounding grace of God. These I do not mind sharing for whatever they may be worth. The reader will find them arranged in relation to the poems they accompany rather than sequentially, although within each section there is a kind of sequence.

A word is in order as to the basis of arrangement. The compilation begins with a group which I have entitled "Deep Rootage," dealing with my old home and early personal backgrounds. The second section, "God Speaks Through His World," reflects mainly the same environs, first with a sequence of the seasons and then with several poems from one of my most beloved resting-places of former years. I have a great love of natural beauty, and it seldom fails to stir in me a sense of God's presence. But our primary approach to God, and our supreme reason for gratitude for grace abundant, is God's self-disclosure through Jesus Christ and the good news

14

which the church is commissioned to bear. So the next section, entitled "Great Days of Our Faith," presents poems on the primary seasons of the Christian year. Then follows a group of memorial tributes to particular people whose lives closely touched mine and were a living witness to their Christian faith and devotion. I have long believed that the personal and the social Christian message must be blended in an indissoluble union. The next section, therefore, contains social action poems, some old, some new, with numerous observations on the current scene. The final section, entitled "Variant Moods," reflects both trouble and triumph in the Christian's quest, not only my own but, I believe, that of others also.

So this is my witness to the grace of God at home and in Christ's church, at work and at rest, amid nature's beauty and in fellowship with other Christians, in the quest for a better world and in moods of both discouragement and hope. This abundant grace has upheld me in dark days and steadied me in lighter ones. It was available to John Bunyan in his time, and it has abounded to hosts of others. No one can convince me that in our time it will not still abound, if only we will lift up our hearts to discern it.

Deep Rootage

1. Stump Fence

The lines have fallen for me in pleasant places; yea,
I have a goodly heritage.

> (Ps. 16:6)

Gnarled and old and gray it stands,
Lifting ragged arms to heaven—
Arms that once were tentacles
Questing earth's life-giving leaven.

Flying bird or careless breeze
Dropped some seeds there long ago.
Seeds took root, and fostering Nature
Helped the infant saplings grow.

Saplings grew to towering pines,
Spreading mighty arms in pride;
Straight they stood, in poise majestic,
Landmarks to the country-side.

Settlers came and tilled the soil,
Doughty spirits, pioneering.
Trees to them were stuff for houses,
Must be felled to make a clearing.

Thrifty were those early farmers—
Saw that stumps could mark a field.
Oxen tugged. With pull titanic
Beast made earth give up its yield.

Side by side the settlers placed them,
Roots tip-tilted in the air.
Prone they lay, their glory humbled,
Shorn of grandeur, stark and bare.

Long ago the earth they conquered
Has received the pioneers;
But the stump fence stands unvanquished,
Guarding borders through the years.

In current society there is a very ambiguous attitude toward the past. With one part of the modern mind deference is paid to our heritage. On state occasions famous words of freedom, whether from the Declaration of Independence, Lincoln's Gettysburg or Second Inaugural Address, or some hallowed words of scripture, are likely to be quoted. Centennials and other special days of remembrance are observed. In churches the members of the various denominations pay deference, at least occasionally, to their "founding fathers," whether Martin Luther, John Calvin, John Wesley, or many another. The great days of the Christian year derive their greatness, when thoughtfully observed, from the recollection of the events which brought them into being. Devoid of such remembrance, Christmas, Good Friday, and Easter become secular holidays, not days of holy meaning, and this is even more conspicuously true of such days of national observance as Memorial Day, Independence Day, and Thanksgiving.

All this remembrance is good, and the fact that it continues, even though sporadically, gives evidence that our society has not given itself over wholly to the secular and the contemporary. Yet in between such days of recollection it is largely the new that is accented. New advances in scientific knowledge, new technology, new forms of entertainment, new leisure, new morality, new politics, new economics, new ways of achieving success or status in the world—these are much more the dominant motifs of our day than is the recollection of our heritage.

We are not called upon to live in the past. It would be a serious mistake to try to do so. Yet it is essential that we let the past speak to the present and that we be gratefully mindful always of a goodly heritage.

It is of one aspect of such a past that the old stump fence speaks. The author of these words grew up in the open country in northeastern New York, the great-great-granddaughter of the earliest settler of that little community, which was later to be named Harkness in honor of her grandfather. The big old white farmhouse, built about 1820 and still sturdy after a century and a half of use, has housed six generations of Harknesses, and is still home to me when I return to it.

All around are pleasant acres. These are separated, as such plots must be, by fences to keep

21

the cattle from straying where they should not go, for Robert Frost wisely wrote, "Good fences make good neighbors." Modern wire fences, plain, barbed, or electrically charged, are found in the neighborhood, along with stone walls and an occasional old-time rail fence. Yet most picturesque of all are the few remaining stump fences of that country community, nearly two centuries old but still fulfilling the function for which they were intended.

No longer can stump fences be the primary mode of guarding borders. In many areas of our living there are newer and usually more effective ways of doing. Neither our doing nor our thinking should be tethered to tradition, even though it be a picturesque and well-loved tradition. Yet it would be a sad day for ourselves, our society, and our world if we were to forget to be grateful to those pioneers who laid the foundations on which today we build. Yea, we have a goodly heritage.

We thank thee, O God, for grace abounding in the goodly heritage of faith and fellowship, of culture and community, with which thou hast blessed our lives. We thank thee for hallowed memories and for the lasting gifts to our lives of those who lived long before us. Grant us, we pray thee, the grace, the wisdom, and the courage to carry forward this heritage in ways acceptable to thee. Amen.

2. *Blessedness*

You may have ten thousand tutors in Christ, but you have only one father. . . . The kingdom of God is not a matter of talk, but of power. Choose, then: am I to come to you with a rod in my hand, or in love and a gentle spirit?

(I Cor. 4:15, 20-21 NEB)

To move serenely through each passing year
With naught of haste, nor yet of loitering;
To guard in memory the past, and bring
To younger folk its treasury of cheer;
To be a friend to life and know no fear
Of realms beyond its rim; to find no sting
In Fortune's thrusts but good in everything—
This is the life of one I hold most dear.

If I might greet the sunset with this calm,
Find interest in persons, places, books,
And live my eighties in such kindliness,
I should not fear old age. There would be balm
For lessened strength, a gentle grace that looks
Undimmed upon the years—and blessedness.

When Paul wrote to the Corinthian church the words quoted above, he was referring to himself as a spiritual father. He wanted to tell

23

the Christians whom he had had to rebuke for their self-importance and frequent defiance of his counsel that he still loved them as a father. Yet his words indicate the precious character of the fatherly relation, whether spiritual or biological. The question he puts at the end of the passage shows clearly enough that he knew, and believed that they knew, whether the rod or love in a spirit of gentleness was the better way with fathers.

These words are still relevant today, especially in times that accent the generation gap. Granted that there are good fathers who are not Christians and that that some who think of themselves as Christians are not regarded by their offspring as good fathers, the gospel of Christ has more than a little bearing on true fatherhood.

But what of the sonnet to my own father, which was originally written with the subtitle "whose eighty-six years are a virile poem"? What I shall say must inevitably be quite personal, for I owe more to him than to any other person. Not only did he give me his genes to which I owe my good health and long life, but much besides. He saw to it that I had a better education than country girls in those days usually received, and from my earliest memories he shared with me an interest in "persons, places, books," and much else that has blessed my life.

My father lived all his life as a country

farmer. He was also a land surveyor who ran the lines for the countryside, a notary public who drew up many legal documents for his neighbors, and a local historian who had an amazing knowledge of the old roads, bridges and fords, plots of land, and adventures of the early settlers of the community. Intuitively he had an interesting way of speaking and writing about such matters, and fortunately much has been preserved through articles he wrote for the local newspapers. In his earlier years he taught in rural schools winters and worked the farm summers, but this antedates my memory.

Had the opportunities of today, or even a wider environment in his own time, been open to my father he could have gone far. As it was, his influence went deep. As a young man he made a considerable break from his local surroundings to attend Oswego Normal School, now State University College, and he hoped to teach. Just as he graduated, his father died, and as the only son he felt that he must stay home to care for his mother and sisters. I have some of his diaries, and an entry when he was twenty-two tells his life story in embryo: "I am sitting at the old table near the old stove, in the old room where I have sat so many, many times, and the old home seems dear to me tonight though I often think that I had rather be away, out in the world 'fighting life's battles and winning life's victories.' Here I was born,

25

here I have grown to be a man, and here one year ago today my father died, and here I should love to live and die if I thought that I could here be as useful to God, to the world, and to my fellowmen as anywhere else."

When he died in the same old home at the age of eighty-eight, beloved by all the countryside, whatever might be said of his influence in the world, none could doubt his usefulness to God and to his fellowmen. One of my own high moments was when some of our old neighbors and longtime friends recently placed in the church he loved a bronze plaque bearing the inscription, "To the memory of J. Warren Harkness, historian and religious leader, 1848-1937."

In our home we did not talk much about religion. There was a Scotch-Irish taciturnity in our background which made us hesitate to say much about what lay deepest in us. Yet we attended church as regularly as Sunday came around, first in the schoolhouse where services were held with no church-state relations to disturb us, and later in the little Harkness Methodist Church. For many years my father was its unofficial lay leader. Except when he was away at school, he taught a Sunday school class from the age of sixteen to eighty-four. I wonder who else has taught his neighbors for sixty-eight years in the same community!

The poem quoted was written many years

ago. Now I can say the same though in a different tense, and I thank God for my father with a gratitude that cannot be fitly spoken.

Said Paul, "You may have ten thousand tutors in Christ, but you have only one father." True enough, but when a father in a home is at the same time one's foremost guide in Christ, how great the blessing!

Dear Lord and Father of mankind, forgive our foolish ways. We thank thee for grace abounding in our lives through our homes. May the fathers of many households become fathers in Christ through the gospel, and through such fidelity may their children find blessedness. Amen.

3. Eucharist

Her children rise up and call her blessed;
    her husband also, and he praises her.
              (Prov. 31:28)

Upon the dust of one I love
   I place my reddest flower;
Naught else so well bespeaks her life,
   Her deep, enduring power.

Orchid and saffron tell their tale
   Of kindly, gentle grace;
The white is like her stainless self—
   These tenderly I place.

27

> *But in my reddest, richest flower,*
> *Deep crimson, twilight-kissed,*
> *Is writ the travail of her love—*
> *A holy Eucharist.*

These words were written as a tribute to my mother. After I had spoken at some church function, a flower-lover who specialized in gladiolus production sent me several dozen. It seemed appropriate to place a blood-red one upon her grave in our country cemetery.

There is less to say about my mother than my father, for her life was more circumscribed. She had neither his physical stamina nor his breadth of interests. Her contributions were in loving self-giving and patient endurance of suffering rather than in conspicuous creativity.

Forced by illness due to a fall to stop school at the eighth grade, she was married at eighteen to my bachelor father, who was nearing thirty. From that time on, her life was centered in him and her children. Contrary to the second line of the proverb quoted, I am afraid her husband did not praise her as much as he should have—he took her fidelity for granted. Yet there was no scolding between them. Fantastic as it may seem, I do not remember having ever heard a sharp family argument between my parents.

My mother was reasonably well most of her life but below par in energy. The sudden death of my seventeen-year-old sister when I was five —my own first encounter with death—took a severe toll of my mother's strength for many months. In the flu epidemic of 1918 I was very ill, and she nursed me around the clock and probably saved my life, but she was never well after that time. When she died after some ten years of lingering illness, the deep lines of suffering on her face were in sharp contrast to the fresh beauty of her wedding picutre.

Yet what my mother lacked in breadth of outreach, she more than made up in simple goodness. Next to her family, her devotion was to the church. Though she took no such leadership as my father, she was always there when a service was held, and she saw to it that we were there also. I began going to church much longer ago than I can remember, and contrary to the common idea that this inhibits later church-going, I have been going to church ever since!

My mother's devotion to her family went deep —how deep I did not fully realize until I was a woman grown. When the cost of graduate study was more than my slender earnings could supply, it was she who found the money through a modest inheritance from her parents. She could have used it to make her own life more comfortable, but that was not her way. When some family circumstances made it seem that I ought to give up my public career and come home to be with my parents, it was she who insisted that I "had my own life to live" and must not do so.

Such sacrificial self-giving has long been the way of mothers. I have been richly, though not singularly, blessed. But since it is the way of mothers, should we not gratefully, humbly thank God for it? And should we not render our tribute, not in words only, but in living worthily in response to what has been given? The final words of the book of Proverbs say it for us:

Charm is deceitful, and beauty is vain,
    but a woman who fears the Lord is to be praised.
Give her of the fruit of her hands,
    and let her works praise her in the gates.

Lord, we thank thee for mothers. May our lives show forth our gratitude for the grace abounding in them. Amen.

4. God of the Fertile Fields

Thou dost cause the grass to grow for the cattle,
    and plants for man to cultivate,
that he may bring forth food from the earth, . . .
    and bread to strengthen man's heart.
                        (Ps. 104:14, 15b)

God of the fertile fields,
Lord of the earth that yields
  Our daily bread;
Forth from Thy bounteous hand
Come gifts Thy love has planned
That men through all the land
  Be clothed and fed.

We would Thy stewards be,
Holding in trust from thee
  All Thou dost give;
Help us in love to share,
Teach us like Thee to care,
That earth may all be fair
  And men may live.

As grows the hidden seed
To fruit that serves men's need,
  Thy Kingdom grows.
So let our toil be used,
No gift of Thine abused,
No humblest task refused,
  Thy love bestows.

God of the countryside,
Dear to our Lord who died
  To make men one;
We pledge our lives to Thee,
To serve Thee faithfully
Till in eternity
  Our day is done.[1]

[1] Copyright 1955 by the Hymn Society of America.
The Hymn Society suggests "Kirby Bedon" 6.6.4.6.6.6.4.
as its tune. It obviously follows the same metrical setting
as "America."

31

The Hymn Society of America frequently conducts contests to secure new hymns on particular themes. The above verses, submitted in response to a request for rural hymns, were fortunate enough to secure an award. When along with others this hymn was presented in a national television program, the announcer stated that its author had never lived on a farm. How wrong he was!

God is still God of the fertile fields, though there are serious problems today in agriculture and in the life of rural America. Farm machinery has become indispensable, and this the small farmer often cannot afford to buy. Meanwhile his living costs increase more rapidly than any profits received from his produce. The large farms and ranches appear to be lucrative, but often at the cost of employing human labor, especially "stoop-labor," for handpicking of what the machines cannot handle. Such persons are usually migrants with no settled place in the community and no rights of collective bargaining. We hear much of a crisis in the cities, but there is a rural crisis as well.

As a result many small farmers have given up trying to till "the fertile fields." Their young people, and often their elders, go elsewhere for more assured and better-paid employment. For example, my nephew who lives still on the Harkness acres rents them out to a neighbor and commutes nearly fifty miles daily to and from his job, and none of his three sons has chosen to be a farmer. The barns stand empty, and there are no longer animals to feed or farm chores to do.

I shall not attempt to pass judgment on the economics of the rural situation today. However, in at least two features, a deep stability is still discernible. One of these is a rich and heart-warming neighborliness. Granted that the mobility of the times has made inroads upon it, country people move less often than city dwellers, and as their roots go deeper, their concern for one another is greater. When illness or bereavement strikes, the telephones are busy with the news, and help is offered, sympathy expressed. A country funeral is not a formal thing; it is an occasion at which all the neighbors gather to express by their presence, even without words, their concern for the old friend who has left this life.

The other factor which survives, sometimes weakened but still with more power than weakness, is the neighborhood's rural church. About this I shall say more presently. Yet in any appraisal of the rural situation it must not be overlooked that the church by its very presence is a kind of binding tie that, in spite of social changes, helps hold the community to a common center. Were it to disappear through lack of financial or moral support, I know of nothing that could adequately take its place.

33

I am grateful to God that I grew up amid God's fertile fields in a rural community. While in point of years the greater part of my life has been spent away from the Harkness church and the community around it, they are very dear to me. When I return, as I try to at least once a year, to see my family, preach in the little church, and see my old friends and neighbors who are left, it is one of the high points of my year. The best part of it is that they welcome me, not as a theological seminary professor or the author of books, but as one of them with the mutual enrichment of common memories. They are the salt of the earth, and the salt has not lost its savor.

We thank thee, God, for the fertile fields thou hast given for the sustenance of men. We pray that the fruit of these fields may be gathered and used in stewardship to thee. And we thank thee too for rich offerings to human living from the rural community, the rural home, the rural church. May they go on in strength throughout the changing conditions of our world. Amen.

5. *Benediction*

As each has received a gift, employ it for one another, as good stewards of God's varied grace: whoever speaks, as one who utters oracles of God;

whoever renders service, as one who renders it by the strength which God supplies; in order that in everything God may be glorified through Jesus Christ. To him belong glory and dominion for ever and ever. Amen.

(I Pet. 4:10-11)

Beloved of all the countryside he is:
With memories that stretch through many a year
He sets the past aglow with life. Good cheer
And kindliness and faith undimmed are his.

The words he speaks are those of gentle grace:
His hand-clasp puts fresh vigor into life.
Amid the things of strain and stress and strife
It gives new peace to look upon his face.

Within his presence pettiness departs:
A benediction rests upon his brow,
And sheds its light serene on those who now
Take up the torch in fellowship of hearts.

The secret of such life I think I know:
God's living presence makes his face to glow.

With this poem about a country minister I wish to say a little more about the rural church which is my home base, and about rural churches in a wider context. It was not written of a rural minister under whose pastorate I grew up but of one in a neighboring community. Yet except for the references which suggest a man well along in years, it could equally well be said of several who have served the Harkness Methodist Church.

We have always been an out-appointment of a nearby village church, for Harkness itself is not a village. It is an open country crossroads with its people living from a few hundred feet to several miles around. Originally there was the West Peru congregation, with a lovely little white church built in the mid-nineteenth century but few members, and the Hallock Hill parish, which met in a schoolhouse until I was sixteen, and it was there that I took my vows of membership. Eventually the two congregations united, moved the church building midway to Harkness, and a little later erected a parish house for church suppers and other functions. Both buildings were immediately dedicated free from debt through voluntary labor and contributions which, for those farmers, were generous ones. This seems unbelievable in our day of heavy mortgages for the erection of church buildings, but it happened.

The salaries in those days were very low, and one wonders now how our ministers existed. Yet they did, and they left their imprint on their people's lives, including mine. They sometimes had less education than would now be required for an appointment; some had their peculiarities. Yet on the whole, they were a succession of faithful men and dedicated servants of God. I owe them much, and their memory is a benediction.

When I used occasionally to attend Troy

Conference, it thrilled me to hear the old ministers sing. One of their favorites was:

> On Jordan's stormy banks I stand,
> And cast a wishful eye
> To Canaan's fair and happy land,
> Where my possessions lie.

To many of them that was where most of their possessions were! Certainly not on this earth, where often they served a lifetime on not more than $2,000 a year, perhaps less, but managed to educate their children and live modestly, yet faithfully, as "good stewards of God's varied grace."

The rural church today is not much sought after. Though salaries are higher and living conditions more comfortable than they once were, they are still below those of most suburban communities, and it is natural that ministers should prefer the latter. I do not condemn them. Yet I thank God the rural church today continues to minister to souls who need its quickening touch. A rural minister—or any other—to serve effectively must love God and must love people. He must render his service "as one who renders it by the strength which God supplies." Let us thank God that there are those who do.

May the God of the fertile fields take pleasure in seed sown in human hearts by dedicated servants, and may this seed continue to bear fruit. Amen.

6. School Days

Happy is the man who finds wisdom,
    and the man who gets understanding,
for the gain from it is better than gain from silver
    and its profit better than gold.

(Prov. 3.13-14)

I have a cupboard full of well-thumbed books—
Greek grammars, lexicons, an Odyssey,
And Caesar's Wars—quite battle-scarred it looks,
In three parts like all Gaul! This history
Was fine on Marathon and Salamis.
Here is Les Miserables. The binding's cheap.
The readers were a bore, but I liked this.
I loved my Virgil—Dido made me weep.

And here's a dull brown-covered one—it seems
It's Elements of English Composition.
Oh, yes! from this we did our daily themes—
Short narratives, and sometimes exposition.

I conned these well, almost each line I knew;
And like old friends, they left their residue.

Since the reader has now been told of the grace abounding in my early home and church environment, he may also wish to know some-
38

thing of my school experiences. This poem, written after coming upon some long-unopened textbooks from my high school days, may suggest something of them.

Until I was twelve, I attended a one-room country school in the same building where we gathered on Sunday for worship. It was a Protestant community, and the one Roman Catholic family were friendly neighbors who made no objection. The recent increase in ecumenical friendliness was antedated years ago, for in our community there was mutual respect and no quarreling between churches.

When I had advanced far enough to pass my Regents' examinations in the basic subjects, I entered Keeseville High School, five miles away. At first my brother and I drove back and forth—not in an automobile, for those were "horse and buggy" days. But before long it seemed best to stay down through the week, taking our provisions with us for the coming week and returning Friday night for my mother and me to cook our staples on Saturday for the following one. In the meantime we stayed at Aunt Sallie's—not a relative but a kind of "universal aunt" who thus harbored for a pittance a long succession of country boys and girls as they attended high school. I think we paid two dollars a month per person!

I owe much to those high school years, but two things in particular have "left their residue."

One of these is the way the teachers encouraged my love of learning, made what I studied come alive, and saw to it that I was prepared for college. A Greek class was started of which I was the only member, and I ate up my four years of Latin. Now little Latin and less Greek are studied in high schools. It is doubtless better to have more subjects geared to the modern world, yet the departure of the classics is a lost legacy.

The second main contribution of the high school years came from the village church. We were not there on Sunday, but my room-mate and I—it sounds archaic to say it!—attended Wednesday night prayer meeting quite regularly. Also, when there were evangelistic meetings, as there usually were for a time each winter, we got our studying done in time to attend most of them. It was in one of these that I made my basic commitment to Christ. Whether it should be called conversion depends on the meaning given to the term. I felt no great upheaval of soul, but I did feel that from then on I must be a Christian. I well remember my mingled fright and exultation when I gave my first public testimony, and soon after that I joined the church. Try as I may, I cannot remember the traveling evangelist's name, but doubtless God knows and has granted him his reward.

So, in ways not then foreseen, I was being prepared for living later in a far different world.

And I thank God with fullness of heart for the richness of those early days.

Accept, O God, our tributes of remembrance and thanksgiving. And help us go forward in service to thee as we remember those long since taken to thy nearer presence. Amen.

7. Permanence

The grass withers, the flower fades;
> but the word of our God will stand for ever.
>> (Isa. 40:8)

> *I dwell in a house that used to be,*
> *A house that now is gone:*
> *Where friendly walls and columns stood*
> *There grows a fresh green lawn.*

> *It was in the way: they tore it down:*
> *They carried it off in carts.*
> *But they could not carry away the things*
> *Time builds within our hearts.*

> *The memories of youthful dreams,*
> *Of friendship and of song,*
> *These live, and still will live when I,*
> *Like it, to earth belong.*

The village of Keeseville, where I attended high school, is now only a few minutes by car from the ancestral home. I have been there many times, but once in particular I felt impelled to go down a bystreet and take a look at what had been Aunt Sallie's house, though I knew she was no longer living. The above bit of verse tells my thoughts as I discovered that there was nothing there but a well-kept lawn, an adjunct to another piece of property.

This is a little parable of the state of affairs in our world, where the new comes swiftly and often unexpectedly. Much that I have told about in the preceding pages belongs to a vanished world, and if by chance this should be read by any young person, it must sound antediluvian. The changes that have taken place in the twentieth century in geometrical progression to all that went before are as fantastic as any science fiction, and it is a wonderful century in which to have lived.

Yet there are some things that do not change. Among them are nobility of character, integrity, loving self-giving, fidelity to duty, generosity, kindliness, an outgoing concern for others. These are the stable foundations of any era. Is there more or less of them today? This is a useless question, for such things cannot be measured quantitatively. Apparently both these qualities and their opposites can be found at any period of history.

The Christian church exists to accent such qualities through the gospel of Christ. This is not its only goal; it exists also to glorify God —to render to God praise and thanksgiving for his abounding grace. Say, if we will, that this is the "chief end" of man and of the church, it still is true that we glorify God by demonstrating such qualities in ourselves and helping others to achieve them.

I do not despair of the church today. Like the society all around it, it has changed greatly within one person's memory. In spite of what the critics are fond of saying, I believe most of these changes are for the better. Though I have heard so much about "relevance" and "irrelevance" that the terms leave me slightly nauseated, if one must use them I believe that the church is more relevant to human need today than it has ever been. There is hope-inspiring wisdom in the words of Jesus to Peter, "On this rock I will build my church, and the powers of death shall not prevail against it" (Matt. 16:18).

The church exists both to strengthen and quicken the inner life of man and to help create a better society. Of the latter function we shall say more later. Neither of these aims should preempt the place of the other, for they belong together. But let us not forget that plain, simple, down-to-earth *goodness* is one of the pillars on which society must rest.

Such goodness will endure because God endures. So, whatever changes may come to sweep

43

away old landmarks, let us not despair. God lives, Christ lives, the church which is the carrier of Christ's gospel lives, goodness lives. All of these will endure to the end of time, and beyond it to eternity.

We thank thee, O God, that thy word of promise endures to all generations. Help us amid the changing scenes of our time to know that thou art strong and loving and secure, and in this faith may we go forward in hope and love. Amen.

God
Speaks Through
His World

8. Dayspring

For in the tender compassion of our God
  the morning sun from heaven will rise upon us,
to shine on those who live in darkness, under the
    cloud of death,
  and to guide our feet into the way of peace.
              (Luke 1:78-79 NEB)

Late it comes. Rising in golden majesty
Over the feathery, tree-capped eastern hill,
The sun appears. It throws triumphantly
White gleams across the field, snow-clad and
    still.
On tree and shrub, on every stick and stone
Lightly lies a glistening counterpane.
Against the sky a haystack, bleak and lone,
Stands sharply lined. Upon the wind-swept
    plain
Snow-fences raise their firm, red lattice-work.
A row of maples, bare and gnarled and hoary,
And farther on the steeple of the kirk
Lift up their heads to greet the sunshine's glory.

From snow-roofed cottages, blue threads of
    smoke
Curl lazily to meet the pearl-gray sky,
And fade away. Here sturdy farmer folk
Perform their tasks and let the days go by.
This scene serene, remote from sound of strife
Bespeaks the peace of God, the Lord of life.

47

As long as I had my parents, I went home every Christmas to be with them for at least a few days, though my work kept me elsewhere the greater part of the year. This verse describes a winter sunrise in that rural setting.

The words from the Bible are from Zechariah's prophecy at the birth of his son who was to be known throughout the Christian world as the forerunner of Christ, "the dayspring from on high." The older translation may have left us unaware that "dayspring" means simply sunrise, a term that suggests the coming of light and peace. So while the poem does not mention Jesus, even so common a thing as a sunrise suggests what God has done for the world both through the realm of nature and the realm of grace.

In theological circles there has been a considerable fluctuation in the emphasis given to these two realms. The liberalism of the early part of this century laid strong emphasis on the life and teachings of Jesus but also on the agreement between religion and science if we will view the laws of nature as the laws of God, God's manifold ways of working within his world. Then came Barthian neo-orthodoxy and the tendency to think of God's revelation through Christ, with the Bible and the church its mediating channels, as the only real source of our knowledge of God. Now the pendulum has swung again to the immanence of God in physical and human nature, with an accent on God's self-disclosure through beauty and sensory experience as well as through the human struggle to make this a better world for all to live in.

"God fulfils himself in many ways," wrote the poet Tennyson. And another poet of the nineteenth century, William Cullen Bryant, paid tribute to God's presence in nature without using the word God when he wrote:

> To him who in the love of Nature holds
> Communion with her visible forms, she speaks
> A various language: for his gayer hours
> She has a voice of gladness, and a smile
> And eloquence of beauty; and she glides
> Into his darker musings with a mild
> And healing sympathy, that steals away
> Their sharpness, ere he is aware.[2]

These words are profoundly true. And because they are true, though God is to be found supremely in Jesus, the dayspring who is the bearer of eternal light, God is to be found also in a sunrise. *Any* sunrise, anywhere, but when it is within the peace and beauty of a snow-clad countryside, how eloquently it speaks! No wonder the greeting cards so often use country snow scenes as their setting for Christmas cheer!

[2] The opening words of "Thanatopsis." Though the main theme of the poem is death, it speaks benignly of life.

We thank thee, God, with joy and gladness mingled with deep solemnity for the dayspring from on high that has visited us in thy Son. And we bless thee too that in the beauty of thy world thou hast given us a quickening witness to thy goodness and abounding grace. Amen.

9. *The Strength of the Hills Is His ʌlso*

In his hand are the deep places of the earth: the strength of the hills is his also.

(Ps. 95:4 KJV)

I lift up my eyes to the hills.
　From whence does my help come?
My help comes from the Lord,
　who made heaven and earth.

(Ps. 121:1-2)

Around me all is murky mud
　And springtime freshets flow,
For here the frost is going out—
　But on the hills is snow!

Across an opalescent lake
　They tower, jagged, high,
Gray, lapis, azure, turquoise, mauve,
　Snow-capped against the sky.

I look around at the muddy earth:
　I think of earthy things.
I lift my eyes up to the hills:
　My spirit then takes wings!

The poem preceding this describes a winter sunrise. Since I wish to present a sequence of the seasons, this one has a spring setting. But not in the usual mood of spring, with singing birds and bursting flowers. The setting here is mud, plain mud.

During my years of college teaching, it was standard practice to have a week's vacation at Easter time, and I went home for it. Depending on the variable date of Easter and the particular quirks of that year's weather, it could still be winter, or the beginnings of a settled spring, or in between. At this intermediate stage the roads, some of them hard-surfaced but more of them not, could be precarious with deep ruts and oozing mud.

But the hills! They were glorious to behold. I grew up amid the foothills of the Adirondack mountains. What we had near us were hills, some rolling, some jagged, some covered with evergreens, some with glacial moraine from long ago cropping out in the midst of what in summer would be a grassy slope. At any time of year they were lovely. In the spring when the frost was going out, the hills were usually still snow-clad, and as the sun shone on them, one could see a kaleidoscopic mass of color. With good reason the chapel of Middlebury College on the Vermont side of Lake Champlain bears against its own gleaming whiteness the inscription, "The strength of the hills is his also."

51

In this juxtaposition of hills and mud there is a little parable of human existence. Much of our living is muddied with the humdrum demands of every day. Some of it is inevitably tear-stained as one cruel circumstance after another falls upon suffering humanity. So prevalent is this aspect of existence that in some minds Christian faith has been replaced by a philosophy of the absurd which sees no meaning in human life or in the universe. But the hills are still there if we will lift up our eyes.

To the psalmist the hills spoke of God, and therefore of strength and joy. Many times he writes about them. "The hills gird themselves with joy" (65:12). "Let the floods clap their hands; let the hills sing for joy together before the Lord, for he comes to rule the earth" (98:8-9). "The mountains skipped like rams, the hills like lambs" (114:4). Such passages, and many others, praise the Lord, the maker of all. In Ps. 121:1 the older version is "I will lift up mine eyes unto the hills, from whence cometh my help." Doubtless the Revised Standard is more accurate, but either form speaks to our hearts, for the Lord who made the hills imparts to us his joy and strength.

Help us, O thou Lord of our world, to remember that amid the mud and scum of things, there always, always something sings. Amen.

10. God's Clarion

Be still before the Lord, and wait patiently for him.
(Ps. 37:7)

> . . . he makes me lie down in green
> pastures.
> He leads me beside still waters;
> he restores my soul.
>
> (Ps. 23:2-3a)

God of the evening wind, kissing my hair!
God of cicadas, God of the goldenrod!
Glad God that makes of earth's beauty a stair
Whereon I may mount, up and up, through the air
Up to the clouds where the angels have trod—

Angels that peopled my child-world with light
Only to fade in the glare of plain day;
But now I recapture them, cloud-girt and bright,
In the song of cicadas that chant their delight
And my ears are unstopped as they carol their lay.

God of the evening star, shining quick clear!
God of mountains of sable, clouds of rose, gray
*   and tan!*
In the hush of the evening a clarion I hear
To rest and to work again—God's chanticleer—
And in the cool quiet I answer, "I can!"

In the early days of my seminary teaching at Garrett, my usual good supply of energy became greatly depleted. I know in retrospect that there were sufficient reasons for being so tired.

I was determined to do the best work possible in my new job as professor of applied theology— a pioneering post for a woman to hold. By this time the Christian world was extending more invitations to speak and to serve on various committees than it was possible to accept in fairness to my main work, and I had not yet learned to say no. And as if these dual demands on the adrenalin were not enough, an injury to my back kept me in almost constant pain, and the expensive physicians I sought out were more frustrating than helpful.

But what of this poem about a summer evening? When I went home for the summer vacation, I hoped to get rested, but anxiety and tension superseded rest. I wondered seriously whether I could "make it" to go on with the unusual opportunities that had so marvelously been opened to me. Must I simply quit and retreat into some undefined and unknown limbo? I did not know.

I well remember going for a walk one evening after supper, sitting down on a flat stone that had fallen off the stone wall, and giving myself up to the calm beauty of the evening. I do not recall that I thought about the anxieties that confronted me—those were for the hours of insomnia in the night seasons. I simply lost myself in the loveliness of God's world. The words of this poem formed themselves in my mind, and when the dark came, I went to my

54

room and wrote them down. That night I slept well.

By fall I had pulled out of much of the fatigue and the depression that went with it. The renewal of strength and the mastery of my problems did not come all at once, but they came. Three things made this possible. The first was the love of understanding friends. The second was the challenge of a work worth doing. The third was the restorative power of nature. And, throughout and undergirding all of these, God's abounding grace.

So I went back to my duties with zest, and no longer with any fear of failure. Among my students of that period are some of my warmest friends today, and I take great satisfaction in their achievements and service to God and the world. Within a year or two my publishers brought out *The Dark Night of the Soul,*[3] and it is, of course, an open secret that I should not have thought of writing it if I had not gone through this experience. One of my wisest older friends summed it up by saying, "You took a bad thing and made some good come out of it." Perhaps so, but if this be true, it is because God, through loving friends and challenging work and the goodness of his world, made it possible.

So what of this poem about a summer eve-

[3] (Nashville: Abingdon Press, 1945; Apex edition, 1968.)

ning? I do not claim that the sounds and silences of that evening "did the trick." There was no miraculous release from pain either physical or mental. In fact, some of the physical pain from that old injury is still with me and doubtless always will be. While I do not discredit the fact that miracles of healing do sometimes occur, God's ways of coping with a physical disorder are usually the slower ones knit into the total fabric of one's being, and this is often the case with mental troubles as well. Nevertheless, this evening lingers vividly in my memory as a turning point toward new confidence and strength, and it will forever be associated in my mind with the poem's last two words.

O God of the world around us, God of the strange world within us, help us to yield ourselves to thee. Purge us of pride; help us to put away anxiety; stir us anew to rest in thee. For so shall the souls of men be restored, and our world brought nearer to thy good design. Amen.

11. *Cloth of Gold*

Sing, O heavens, for the Lord has done it;
    shout, O depths of the earth;
break forth into singing, O mountains,
    O forest, and every tree in it!
                    (Isa. 44:23)

On a hillside in the soft haze of October,
I beheld a tapestried pattern woven
In old gold and crimson, in scarlet and saffron,
  Telling God's story.

As in days long gone the exploits of heroes
On a cloth of gold were emblazoned in beauty,
In the trees is written the tale of the ages,
  Singing God's glory.

In various travels in Europe or the Orient I have been guided through palaces, temples, or museums, and with fellow tourists have stopped to admire some fine piece of tapestry. Like many Americans I have admired it, then passed on to the next art treasure with only a casual recollection of the preceding one. Were I a connoisseur in such fields, the admiration and the recollection would, of course, be far more vivid.

But the trees of autumn! Never does their flaming beauty fail to thrill me. Whether among my native hills or elsewhere, the fall foliage speaks to me of God and the beauty of his handiwork. This verse was written in central New York, where I taught philosophy and religion for fifteen years at Elmira College.

There are a good many passages in the Bible, especially in the psalms but also elsewhere, which declare the beauty and strength of nature, thereby ascribing glory to God who is its maker. Yet as far as I know, God is never referred to in the Bible as the divine Artist. Creator, Judge,

57

Redeemer, Guide, Defender, Father—these and many other symbols speak of the Most High. Yet the note of God as fashioner and lover of the beautiful is considerably muted in biblical theology, much more so than with the Greeks.

There are reasons why this is so. To the Old Testament mind the beauty of holiness far surpassed the holiness of beauty. Idolatry must be guarded against at all costs, for God alone is Redeemer and Lord. However, in a book of the Apocrypha, the Wisdom of Solomon, this warning takes a fresh turn, for the rejection of idolatry is linked with the beauty of God's world as evidence of its Creator. Of fire, wind, water, and the heavenly bodies the author says:

And if it was through delight in their beauty that they took them to be gods,
Let them know how much better than these is their Sovereign Lord;
For the first author of beauty created them:
But if it was through astonishment at their power and influence,
Let them understand from them how much more powerful is he that formed them;
For from the greatness of the beauty even of created things
In like proportion does man form the image of their first maker. (13:3-5) [4]

[4] (New York: Thomas Nelson and Sons, 1894.) All quotations from the Apocrypha are from this version. The Roman Catholic Church, but not Protestantism, regards the Apocrypha as part of the canonical Scriptures.

In the New Testament it was the love and the goodness of God, and what he required of those who would live according to his purposes, that became the dominant notes. Penitence, divine forgiveness, discipleship, and service in in love to God and neighbor took the place of joy in the beauty of God's world. Yet the human heart must have its meed of beauty. Of this the religious art of all the centuries gives evidence, and in Christian worship at its best, faith, adoration, and beauty blend.

So the Christian finds no barrier to discovering God in the flaming beauty of an autumn hillside. An aesthetic experience? Yes, but a religious one as well. Let us be thankful that at the same time, in one experience, there need be no cleavage between the lifting power of beauty and a response to "the first author of beauty," the supreme Artist of all that is.

We thank thee, God, that thou hast made the earth so fair. Help us to open our eyes to its beauty, and from it to lift our hearts to thee. Amen.

12. My Lake

O Lord, how manifold are thy works!
In wisdom hast thou made them all;
the earth is full of thy creatures.
(Ps. 104:24)

My lake in many moods is seen:
Sometimes with steel-clad, silvery sheen
It flashes boldly in the sun
Like knight with tourney to be won.

And now it seems more like the maid
Whose sleeve he wears—its sylvan shade
Her tresses, veiled with feathery lace—
A jeweled gown, a lovely face.

The mood is changed; the winds blow loud;
My lake is like a charger proud
That plunges fiercely in the fray
And holds the enemy at bay.

When darkness falls, by moonbeams kissed
The knight and maiden keep their tryst.
The stars shine softly overhead
And guard my lake, their nuptial bed.

We come now to a group of poems written
in and about a place which for many years
was very dear to me. Though it now belongs
to the past, any reminder of it brings a flood
of happy memories. Most of these poems are
not specifically religious—but it is hardly necessary always to mention God in order to know
that he is present!

For twenty-five years, from 1931 to 1956, I
had a cottage at Willsboro Bay on Lake Champlain, seventeen miles from the old home. By
this time my mother had died, though my father lived to share it with me for a time. The
sister-in-law who presided over the Harkness

household made my guests welcome, but I did not feel that I should invite them there to add to her labors. The cabin with a lovely lake in front of it, mountains on one side and an exquisite grove of cedars across the bay on the other, and congenial friends in the little community, made it the perfect home away from home.

Here I spent many happy summers, or such parts of the summers as were not taken up with summer school teaching and the inevitable conferences. During those periods I rented the cabin to make it economically profitable. The rest of the time I enjoyed it with my family and the good friends whom I asked to share it with me. There was work, yes, but we did it together, and the occasional crises that came along even in that idyllic spot now seem like pinpricks. After I had moved across the continent and could no longer use the cottage much or look after it personally, I sold it. Its name during all those years was Hate-to-Quit-It, and it was aptly named!

The lake itself was a scene of ever-changing beauty. I do not recall what prompted me to use in this poem symbolism from the age of chivalry in merry England. But I do remember reading it to one of my guests, the professor of classical languages at Elmira College, where I then taught. His comment was, "I like it, all but the end of it." Something indelicate

61

about referring to a nuptial bed! He has now been gone many years, but how dismayed he would be at today's free speaking! A proper balance doubtless lies between the scruples of speech in former years and today's obscenities of both speech and action. The Bible certainly does not hesitate to speak about sex and the marriage bed, but never do we find it or the gospel countenancing the lustful liberties all too common in our time. Perhaps we had better say that sex, like lakes and mountains and cedar trees, is the good gift of God to be used to his praise and glory.

We thank thee, God, for the ever-changing beauty of thy world, for lovely lakes and mountains, for good friends that make life richer, for rest from labor that makes work more zestful. And we thank thee, too, for knights and maidens wedded to each other in happy homes throughout thy fair world. Amen.

13. Sounds

Blessed is the people that know the joyful sound: they shall walk, O Lord, in the light of thy countenance.

(Ps. 89:15 KJV)

Four sounds I hear;
They give me cheer.

A goldfinch trills a lively note
As merry as its yellow throat.

A soft wind gently stirs the trees;
The poplars whisper in the breeze.

The waves strike rhythmically the shore,
And lave good-humoredly its floor.

A cricket is a merry thing—
In rhythmic cadences to sing
His way through hush of evening hours.
He is to sound what cheery flowers
Are to sight in sunshine's glow.
A happy time he has, I know!
I'd like to catch the song he sings,
For crickets are such merry things.

Perhaps the "joyful sound" to which the psalmist refers is limited to the "festal shout" which the Revised Standard Version makes of it. But why should it be? Only four lines earlier the psalmist says, "The heavens are thine, the earth also is thine: as for the world and the fulness thereof, thou hast founded them." Though he says nothing of goldfinches or crickets, surely the joyous sounds within a temple are not the only ones which tell forth the glory of God.

Almost all the sounds of the natural order, like most of the scenes of unspoiled nature, are pleasing ones. An ominous clap of thunder or

63

the rush of destructive winds or waters may cause fear rather than joy. Yet most of the everyday sounds of nature—bird songs, gentle breezes, rustling leaves, babbling brooks, and cascading waterfalls—are pleasant to the ear. So usually are the sounds of playful young animals, whether human or subhuman. It is when man with his technological prowess creates machinery that grinds and thumps, airplanes that cleave the air with a deafening roar, and electronic mass media that seem incessantly to pound the eardrums, that both the silences and the sounds of nature are interrupted. Add to such the sounds of quarreling or of aimlessly loquacious voices, so-called music that sounds more like raucous noise, and the dreadful din of death-dealing guns, and the joyous sounds of nature are no longer present.

This is not to say that progress must stop to keep everything quiet and pleasing to the ear! This could not be if we were to wish for it. Yet perhaps nature—and God speaking through nature—has something to teach us. If so, let us be quiet long enough to hear it.

Our Lord, we would be still and know that thou art God. And in the stillness we would hear thee speak through the sounds of thy untrammeled world. So may we walk forward in the light of thy countenance. Amen.

14. Fairyland and Cathedrals

Praise ye the Lord. Praise ye the Lord from the
heavens: praise him in the heights. . . . Mountains,
and all hills; fruitful trees, and all cedars.

(Ps. 148:1, 9 KJV)

I know a lovely spot where cedars grow,
Symmetrical and tall, a bower of green.
Untouched by human hand it is, I know,
Yet craft of Master-Gardener is seen.
At twilight time I muse amid its shade;
Almost I think I see an elf peep out;
For Nature's witchery has on it laid
Her spell, and cast enchantment all about.
Here might Titania by moonbeams' light
Hold court with Oberon, with flitting Puck
To do the royal bidding—happy sprite!—
And charming Ariel to bring good luck.
The daytime world—how far away it seems!
Such sylvan loveliness was meant for dreams.

———————

The sturdy tillers of the Old World's soil,
Endowed with little goods but rich in love,
Gave freely of their substance and their toil
To lift eternal praise to God above.
They reared cathedrals towering to the skies;
Their craftsmen built in beauty for all time;
In graceful strength the spires and arches rise,
The tracery delicate, the form sublime.
A cathedral of rare artistry I know:
Its Gothic spires, superb in molded line,

65

Point upward gracefully. God made it so,
Its columns exquisite, its art divine,
And living beauty bids me worship where
A grove of cedars forms this place of prayer.

Mention has been made of a lovely grove of cedars not far from the Willsboro Bay cottage. It lay to the right across a small bay, an inlet from the larger one, and a few easy strokes of the oars would transport one to it, and to a world of its own. To speak prosaically, it was pastureland with a fringe of open space in front of a considerable stand of timber, part of a nearby farm. Yet by some spontaneously chosen nomenclature it had long been known as Fairyland. Many were the picnics held there, and at any time of day, but especially at sunset with the sun in its golden glory streaming across the water, it had an unearthly beauty.

It happens that I have two poems which seek to describe this lovely spot, one in Shakespeare imagery appropriate to a dwelling place of fairies, the other in more conventional Christian terms. Not quite sure which to include, I have placed them together to let the reader take his choice. Yet there is more than expediency in this move. For why should not the imagery of fantasy and that of Christian devotion be brought together? Both are an important part of life, and neither need exclude the other.

We hear much in these times about breaking
66

down the walls between the sacred and the secular. With some aspects of this movement I heartily agree; from some others I must dissent. The entire world is God's world. He has "made everything beautiful in its time" (Eccl. 3:11), and things sacred ought not to be set off in a corner by themselves. But what of the rejection or neglect of the Bible as sacred scriptures containing in a special way God's eternal Word, of the church as the carrier of a gospel of unique sacredness, of the transcendent God as the personal Creator of his world? Where these are dropped out in emphasizing the sacredness of the secular world, I cannot go along. This is often done today with the hope of appealing to the secular mind, but it is a mistake. The message we give must be an authentic one with its own distinctive focus, or it will reach nobody.

So let us see the hand of God in "mountains, and all hills; fruitful trees, and all cedars." Let us praise him in whatever way is best suited to our temperament, if the praise has fitness and due reverence. But let us not forget that the earth is the Lord's and the fulness thereof.

Our God, we thank thee that in wisdom and love thou hast placed so much beauty in the world for our happiness and blessing. Help us to use thy good gifts in growth in grace and in service to one another. Amen.

67

15. *Hymn to the Sun*

But for you who fear my name the sun of
righteousness shall rise, with healing in its wings.
You shall go forth leaping like calves from the stall.
(Mal. 4:2)

Thou flaming font of healing might,
Make me, O Sun, thine acolyte!

When after slumber comes the ray
Of new-born light to wake the day,
  Grant me to share thy way.

On wingèd waves through time and space
Thou ridest on with measured pace,
  Grant me to share thy grace.

As thou dost joy to waft to earth
A laughing warmth, a blossoming birth,
  Grant me to share thy mirth.

When twilight's touch hides thee from sight
Still dost thou shine by moonbeams' light,
  Grant me to share thy night.

As men of old have worshiped thee,
Still art thou flaming deity!

It is a daring thing to include this poem. I
can almost hear some reader say, "After all the
author has said about the Christian God, this
is just primitive animism!" One who is familiar
with ancient literature may find here some

echoes of Re, the sun-god of Egypt, or Apollo in the Roman pantheon. Or it may seem like pantheism or at least the pan*en*theism which Bishop John A. T. Robinson espouses, or as the nature mysticism of some exponents of the new theology.

Of these guesses, the one nearest right is the reference to the Egyptian sun-god. The biblical passage quoted from Malachi, according to the great Egyptologist James H. Breasted, shows traces of Egyptian influence, for there the winged disk of the sun was often represented as a source of protection and blessing. Touched by the healing vitality of the sun which the prophet identified with the God of the Hebrews as the sun of righteousness, gloom would be chased away, and one would skip with the exuberance of a calf newly released from its stall.

As a matter of fact, I wrote this poem to express my own feelings of healthy exuberance while lying in the sun at Hate-to-Quit-It. If I did not leap physically like a calf let out of its confinement, something within me did. Theology aside, this is simply a form of address to one of the most elemental forces of nature. I do not think it strange that people in all ages, including the present, have occasionally felt an urge to deify the life-giving rays of the sun. One of the earliest extant devotional classics is the "Hymn to Aton" (another name for the sun-god), which was written in the fourteenth century before Christ by the Pharaoh Akhenaten:

Thou living Aten, the beginning of life!
When thou art risen on the eastern horizon,
Thou hast filled every land with thy beauty. . . .
Thou drivest away the darkness and givest thy rays.[5]

In the present, it is only when one tries to construct a theology which has nature instead of nature's God at its center that error arises.

So if I need to defend myself against heresy, I know as well as anybody that the sun does not hear and answer prayer! But the sun of righteousness, the God of our faith, does. If he wills to do this through the healing rays of the sun and the bounteous nature which is quickened by its warmth, is not this one more occasion of grace abounding?

We thank thee, God, that thou art both the sun of righteousness to heal downcast spirits and the giver of thy quickening sun that warms and nourishes our bodies. May we ever by our living and our speaking, by our working and our resting, render to thee grateful praise. Amen.

[5] Quoted in *Everyday Life in Bible Times* (Washington: National Geographic Society, 1967), p. 124. The spelling used there is "Aten," but "Aton" is the more common form.

16. Moonlight

And God made the two great lights, the greater light to rule the day, and the lesser light to rule the night; he made the stars also. And God set them in the firmament of the heavens to give light upon the earth, to rule over the day and over the night, and to separate the light from the darkness. And God saw that it was good.

(Gen. 1:16-18)

> *Like the cobweb dreams that flit*
> *In beauty by,*
> *So are the feathery clouds*
> *In a moonlight sky.*
>
> *Like a love that flames in the dark*
> *And veils its light,*
> *So is the wordless hush*
> *Of a moonlit night.*

Not only the sun but the moon has always had a strange fascination for people. Sometimes this has been in the direction of assuming that evil influences proceed from it. To this day the word lunatic, literally meaning moonstruck, is in our vocabulary from the assumption of an earlier day that the moon was in some way responsible for serious mental disorders. I do not know when this superstition disappeared, but I do know that in my childhood there were those in our neighborhood who consulted the calendar carefully before butchering the hogs for the winter's meat supply. If the moon was growing, the meat in the frying-pan would remain plump and juicy; if waning, the chops would shrivel and get hard. My parents never adhered to this view, but I remember arguing it with a neighbor, then quitting because neither could convince the other. I learned early that superstitions have a stubborn tenacity that cannot be countered by argument.

Superstition aside, the soft glow of moonlight is most often associated with love and romance. This is not surprising, for moonlight has an unearthly beauty which tends to make the rough spots of existence recede and the lovely side of both things and people come to the foreground. It cultivates intimacy, and intimacy draws the souls and the bodies of lovers together.

Yet romance is not the only sphere on which the moonlight casts its spell. I recall writing the above lines after a marvelous moonlit night at Hate-to-Quit-It when it seemed almost a sacrilege to come back into the house and turn on the electric light with its dream-dispelling glare. Perhaps this is a little parable of much of our existence—the rarest moments of beauty are transient, but they leave their residue in memories that bless and heal. So whether younger or older, let us revel in the moonlight as one more of God's good gifts. "God saw that it was good," and should not we?

But in these days it is not moonlight but the

space race to the moon that gets attention and makes news. We do well to marvel at the conquests of space that have occurred in recent years, and it would be a very dull person who did not feel a lift of spirit from the courage and skill of the astronauts. Insofar as this is for the purpose of acquiring fresh scientific knowledge, some expenditure is justified. Yet I do not myself believe that the vast sums of money now being spent on the race to the moon are nearly so well spent as they would be if used to relieve poverty and misery upon earth. Since the Russians seem to be doing such a good job at space exploration, why not let them do it and have the glory that goes with it? In the meantime we could outdo them in human service to a world in dire need, which might be a better way to glorify both God and ourselves.

But this important matter of political policy and social ethics is not what the poem is about; instead it aims to lift up the simple and encompassing beauty of the moonlight. The enjoyment of this beauty, which when not eclipsed by man-made lights costs nothing except to open our eyes and our souls, is one more evidence of God's abounding grace.

God, we thank thee that thou hast made the world so beautiful. Let our eyes be never dim to its enchantment nor our souls dull to its lifting power. Amen.

17. Miracle

As for me, I would seek God,
and to God would I commit my cause;
who does great things and unsearchable,
marvelous things without number.

(Job 5:8-9)

"Do miracles occur?" I hear men say
As if to probe God's ways in anxious doubt.
A miracle is sunset glow of fading day
With azure hues encircling it about.

A miracle is trees piled high with snow,
Green stalwart sentinels against the sky
But decked with feathery plumage bending low
To kiss the sleeping earth and bid it lie.

A miracle is flashing waves of deepest blue,
Beyond are snow-clad mountains staunch and
  grand;
One almost hears God's angels singing through
To bring good news to all this rugged land.

God made earth beautiful—a miracle of joy;
Such speaking witnesses no doubting can destroy.

A miracle is commonly understood to mean
a suspension or violation of natural laws by an
act of divine intervention. As such, it is thought
to be so out of the ordinary that it must have
a supernatural cause. There has long been a
great difference of opinion both as to the miracle

stories in the Bible and whether miracles occur today. As events taking place without natural causes, miracles tend to be viewed with much skepticism in a science-oriented world.

I do not disparage the attempt to find an answer to this problem, for it is closely related to one's total theological position. However, I believe it is a serious misunderstanding of the basic meaning of miracle to think of it only as a suspension of the normal processes of nature. The word miracle is derived from the Latin *miror*—to marvel at or to view with a sense of wonder. Thus, a miracle is something that calls forth in us awe and wonder, a sense of the mystery and marvel of existence. In short, miracles are God's wonderful works.

If this is what a miracle is, we can leave open in any particular instance the question of whether it is an intervention in the natural order. It could be that, or it could be a natural event of which we do not fully understand the causes. What is important is that it speak to us of God's wonderful works and cause us to bow in wonder and gratitude before him. No natural explanation stands in opposition to the fact that the Creator of all nature "does great things and unsearchable, marvelous things without number."

This poem was written much later than most of the preceding ones, on a winter visit to Lake Tahoe, where for a time I had a cottage after moving to the West Coast and selling Hate-

75

to-Quit-It. But its setting could be in many places. I have always taken much delight in natural beauty and have a good many more poems about scenes in nature than are included in this little volume. But those in this section may stand for all of them as we move on to some different approaches to God's abounding grace.

Not everybody sees God in nature—not even all who feel the marvel and lifting power of it. Probably most of us would not unless we had first found God through other channels, preeminently in Jesus Christ and the church which bears his name. And we might not find him in the church unless we had seen his presence in vital Christians. Accordingly, in the next sections we shall be looking at the great days of the Christian church and at some followers of Christ who in dying have left behind them the fragrance of Christian living.

God the Father Almighty, Maker of heaven and earth, we bow in awe and wonder before thy works. In marvelous orderliness, in stupendous grandeur, in soul-stirring beauty thou hast made thy world. Where thou dost call upon us to participate with thee in the fashioning of an unfinished creation, grant us wisdom and zeal, and where we have marred thy fair would, forgive us, O Lord. Amen.

Great Days
of Our Faith

18. Christmas

Do not be afraid! Listen, I bring you glorious news of great joy which is for all the people. This very day, in David's town, a Savior has been born for you. He is Christ, the Lord. Let this prove it to you: you will find a baby, wrapped up and lying in a manger.

(Luke 2:10-12 Phillips)

Long years ago and far away
A babe, new-born, lay on the hay;
His mother, young and sweet, was near—
With Joseph there she had no fear,
Though dark the night, her travail sore,
Upon that lowly stable floor.

The cattle lowed; the shepherds came;
The angels sang with glad acclaim
To witness to that great event,
The birth of One whom God had sent
To lift the weight of sin and strife
And bring to men peace, joy, and life.

That night was long, long years ago.
It scarcely seems it could be so—
That tale of stable, song and star
With wise men coming from afar
To lay before a baby boy
Their gifts of worship, tribute, joy.

Yet still the songs ring out with cheer,
And gifts are brought from far and near;
The mighty choirs peal out His praise
And little children sing their lays,
For pageant, poetry and light
Retell the tale of that wondrous night.

Men everywhere feel a pulse of joy
In thought of that one baby boy;
Love seems nearer, the world less dark,
The grimness of our times less stark,
And peace, that yet awaits good will,
Seems less remote, though waiting still.

It must be true—that tale of old,
New though a thousand times retold.
The world is rich with wealth of love
Because He came from Heaven above,
Because in a manger that Christmas morn
The Babe of Bethlehem was born.

With this poem we begin a section which aims to celebrate with both joy and solemnity the great days of the Christian year. God reveals himself in many ways, and we have earlier noted signs of grace abounding in a personal heritage and in the turning of the seasons and the beauty of nature. Later we shall look at other evidences of God's goodness. Yet undergirding all these approaches to our knowledge of God is his supreme disclosure in Jesus, man of Nazareth and Christ the Lord. This poem simply retells the familiar Christmas story.

Christians ought to look to Christ for guidance and try to pattern lives upon Jesus and his way of love throughout the year. Yet it lies within the agelong practice of the church to pay tribute to its Lord in a special way on special days. This recurrent rhythm is good, for it keeps us from forgetting and calls us to triumphant celebration. On such days even a largely secular Western world stops its usual course to remember Jesus, and by a persistent, mysterious attraction it is drawn a little closer to the way of life he proclaimed and manifested. The birth of every baby is important, but in view of what it has meant to the world that *this* baby was born, the wonder of it overwhelms us.

In this section it will not be necessary to say much about the circumstances of the writing of the poems, for nearly all of them were written after a moving service of worship had stirred in me the desire to put the timeless message of the day into rhythmic lines and contemporary words. Most of these services were at church, but in the case of Christmas a flood of memories comes back to me. At home with the children lined up to sing "Adeste Fideles" for me, in bed and very ill with the squeaky old gramophone rasping out "Joy to the World," Christmas Eve in India at the Madras Missionary Conference, a concert in Japan with the glorious singing of carols by college students, the contrast between the lovely caroling of my Elmira students

81

and a service at the poor-farm where "The Old Rugged Cross" was what Christmas meant to the old men—but let the reader supply his own memories as he will. Christ is everywhere at Christmas.

We thank thee, Lord, for the heritage of song and jubilation, of warmed hearts and good cheer, that comes with the Christmas season. May its message abide with us until Christmas comes again. Amen.

19. Good Friday

Pilate spoke to them again: "Then what shall I do with the man you call king of the Jews?" They shouted back, "Crucify him!" "Why, what harm has he done?" Pilate asked. They shouted all the louder, "Crucify him!" So Pilate, in his desire to satisfy the mob, released Barabbas to them; and he had Jesus flogged and handed him over to be crucified.

(Mark 15:12-15 NEB)

Were you there?
When they robed him with the mocking scarlet?
When they placed the crown of thorns upon his head?
When they cried out, "Crucify him! Crucify him!"?
When they drove the nails into his quivering flesh?
Were you there?

82

I was not—were you?
Would I have sought to save him, had I been there?
Would I have made my protest to the men in
  power?
Would I have spoken out against the surging mob?
Would I have intervened to stop the cruel beating?
I fear I would not—nor would you.

And so he died.
He died for me. He died for you. He died for all.
No merit mine or yours, so great a gift was given
To show the way to conquer sin by faith and love.
But God was there, transfiguring death to glory
The day Christ died.

A desire often expressed today, especially among the younger clergy, is to be "where the action is." This is good in contrast with the tendency of too many of us to wish to avoid becoming involved in controversial situations. Yet action to be constructive and lasting must have deep motivations and the right goals. None higher has ever been presented to the world than in what happened on the first Good Friday. The ultimate test is whether our work accords with the work of God as this comes to us on the cross.

Reference was made in the last unit to men at a poor-farm (a form of welfare doubtless now superseded) who chose to sing "The Old Rugged Cross" as a Christmas carol. This would hardly be worth mentioning except for a depth of meaning beneath the surface. Christmas and Good Friday are inextricably connected, with a connection that reaches to our untutored intuitions as well as to theology. Save for what Christmas means, the death of one more Jew on a hill outside the city wall would long since have been forgotten. Because it was the death of One whose life and teaching gleam with an unearthly glow, the Western world stops at least briefly to pay him tribute.

Unearthly? Yes, in the sense of radiance that seems to transcend time and space and the limitations of an environment outside the mainstream of events many centuries ago, yet very much down to earth in relation to human sin and suffering and the predicament of man in every period of history.

There are numerous theories of the atonement—of what the death of Jesus did for the saving of the world. I do not go along with the idea that God needed this death to propitiate his wrath or that in the death of this one man punishment was exacted for the sins of the entire world. I should find it hard to worship such a God. Yet in the root sense of at-one-ment—of the reconciliation of man to God, of God's taking the initiative in love to arrest man in his sinful course and lead him to God in inner surrender and outward obedience—the cross makes sense.

The death of Jesus Christ upon the cross gives

us both the pattern and the power for living in every age. As pattern, it shows us that in spite of the worst that dull, malicious, and evil men can do, obedience to the call of God is required of us. As power, it not only reveals but imparts a power not our own and by this power enables the transformation of life. We may not be able to spell out just how this power released on Calvary makes life different, but it is the witness of the centuries that it does. To discover and follow this pattern, enabled by this power, is the most life-transforming, and hence the most important, course any individual or group can take.

O God of love and mercy, who didst send thy Son to live in love among men and in fidelity to die, solemnize us anew with the awfulness and the glory of that day. Too often we have shrunk from the costing demands of love and of fidelity to thy call. Forgive us, Lord, and grant us the power from this day to go forward. Amen.

20. Easter Joy

They said to each other, "Did not our hearts burn within us while he talked to us on the road, while he opened to us the scriptures?" And they rose that same hour and returned to Jerusalem; and they found the eleven gathered together and those who

85

were with them, who said, "The Lord is risen indeed, and has appeared to Simon!" Then they told what had happened on the road, and how he was known to them in the breaking of the bread.
(Luke 24:32-35)

Christ the Lord is risen today—
In flowers that burst the bonds of winter's snow
To come, all heaven-decked, to earth below
And make the gladness in our hearts to glow!
Alleluia!

Christ the Lord is risen today—
In mercies manifold that gird our life—
Love, laughter, joy—thy bounties rife
That gleam above the anguish and the strife!
Alleluia!

Christ the Lord is risen today—
In love that spans the miles of swirling sea
To bear our loved ones up and keep them free.
True, strong and fearless may they rest in thee!
Alleluia!

Christ the Lord is risen today—
In thy dear Son thou gavest man to save
From sin and death, from darkness of the grave.
Because He rose, our hearts again are brave!
Alleluia!

The familiar words from the end of the story of the walk to Emmaus have been selected for quoting from the many on the Resurrection in the New Testament because they touch us so intimately where we live. It is in such ordinary
86

matters as a journey on the highway or sitting down to eat together that the presence of the living Christ should make a difference in our living. Otherwise, the Easter jubilation may not strike home very deeply.

The poem was written in wartime; this is the point of the reference to loved ones across the sea. Yet in days of trouble and anxiety or those more placid, the Easter message of joy and hope because of God's victory over sin and death is one that never wears out. May the trumpets continue to sound in our hearts!

It is, of course, not essential that trumpets should sound in every Easter service, though if well used this symbol is appropriate. What is essential is that the day should speak so vitally of God's triumph that Easter becomes the other side of Good Friday—this time with the solemnity of a God-given joy and confident assurance. As Christmas and Easter are inseparably connected, so are Good Friday and Easter. The latter connection is the more obvious, for the time span is less both in the life of Jesus and in the observance of the days. Yet all three are pivotal points in the great Christian drama of redemption. Leave out any of them, and something vital is lost from the other two.

One of the surest marks of a secular society is what it does with Easter. That Easter should have become associated with flowers and the new life of springtime is not strange, for one

87

finds a spring festival in other religions. If this is not allowed to overshadow the deeper meaning, it amalgamates well enough with the Easter message. Nor should I wish to deprive children of the pleasure they get from their egg rolling, Easter bunnies, and other traditions of the day. Yet when such observances as these, plus a lavish display of Easter finery, are substituted for the Christian meaning of Easter, we have moved far toward a collapse of faith in God's triumph over death and evil. A transient pleasure then replaces Easter joy, and because there is no vista of eternity, this life loses much of its deeper meaning. If this tragedy is to be prevented or its advance checked in our society, the churches must reach beneath the surface observances of Easter to the foundations of an enduring joy.

Lord, keep us from forgetting thy gift of Easter joy in the humdrum and ordinary days of our living. And when death or deep trouble comes upon us, help us to be lifted and made strong by the assurance that in thy victory over evil we can triumph also. To thee we render the joyous tribute of grateful hearts. Amen.

21. Easter Mandate

And Jesus came and said to them, "All authority in heaven and on earth has been given to me.

Go therefore and make disciples of all nations, baptizing them in the name of the Father and of the Son and of the Holy Spirit, teaching them to observe all that I have commanded you; and lo, I am with you always, to the close of the age." (Matt. 28:18-20)

Jesus came and stood among them and said to them, "Peace be with you." When he had said this, he showed them his hands and his side. Then the disciples were glad when they saw the Lord. Jesus said to them again, "Peace be with you. As the Father has sent me, even so I send you." (John 20:19*b*-21)

Our Lord Christ died that men might greatly live
And rose triumphant over death and shame.
He speaks again, "Be not afraid. Go give
My message to a waiting world. Proclaim
That He who died is ever by your side
To give God's strength until sin's warfare cease.
My peace be with you." Still these words abide
To bless a stricken world that knows no peace.

Yet with this gift of peace come high demands—
To go and make disciples, teach His way,
To bring the living Word to many lands
Till all shall live in love beneath its sway.

Our Easter alleluias now we raise,
And may our deeds, O Lord, show forth thy praise.

As may be expected in view of the fact that the records were written long after the event,

there are variations in the four Gospels as to
what took place after the Resurrection. Matthew
indicates that Jesus told the disciples to meet
him in Galilee, and it was on a mountain there
that he gave the Great Commission. John places
the first post-Resurrection appearance to them
in Jerusalem in a house where the disciples had
met behind closed doors on the evening of
the first Easter.

The instructions given on these two occasions
were not quite identical, but fully consistent.
"Go tell" and "I send you"—by either word we
have a mission and a mandate. And after these
many centuries the mandate has not expired.

The carrying of the gospel message is a prime
concern of the church, and always has been
when the church has been vigorous and vital.
This is true whether in the local scene or its
wider missionary outreach. In the early days
this witness meant persecution and often death
at the hands of hostile "principalities and powers." Yet those first disciples refused to be silent,
and with a marvelous persistence in spite of
every kind of hardship they carried the Easter
faith to lands far beyond that of its birth. They
pressed forward across continents and oceans,
and their successors carried the faith to western
and northern Europe and eventually to the
Americas. We thus became the recipients of
that heritage. Then from this base it was carried

90

by many a dedicated missionary to Asia, Africa, and the islands of the seas.

The story of the spread of the gospel through its ever-expanding outreach is a great saga of courage and Christian devotion. The missionary movement has been marred at times by a blend of religion with political and cultural imperialism and occasionally by bigotry and other human frailties in its exponents. Yet these are not its primary notes. All in all, it has been a remarkably selfless and Christ-centered enterprise. Whether the missions were Roman Catholic or Protestant, the world has never witnessed a more unselfish giving of life for others. The contributions have been of incalculable value.

The mood and the methods are now changing. In the present "global village" we no longer distinguish as sharply as formerly between home and foreign missions. In response both to rising currents of nationalism in many lands and to a sense of fitness in the carrying of the gospel, this is placed more and more in the hands of Christians of those lands. The presence of these able leaders at ecumenical gatherings is an invigorating witness to its power. Furthermore, emphasis on the ministry of the laity places mission in every aspect of the church's life. So let us not lose hope!

Lord, make me a witness to thy gospel in all my speaking and my living. Amen.

22. How Do I Know?

These things I have spoken to you, while I am still with you. But the Counselor, the Holy Spirit, whom the Father will send in my name, he will teach you all things, and bring to your remembrance all that I have said to you. Peace I leave with you; my peace I give to you; not as the world gives do I give to you. Let not your hearts be troubled, neither let them be afraid.

(John 14:25-27)

How do I know Christ rose on Easter day?
Because He walks beside me in the way.

How do I know our dear ones live again?
Because God's love has promised this to men.

How do I know of victory over sin?
Because His radiance lets the light shine in.

How do I know a hope that nothing can destroy?
Because our world still sings of Easter joy.

How can I know this joy will not depart?
Because He dwells right here within my heart.

The miracle of the Resurrection was no ordinary occurrence. It was apparently one of its kind, and the aura of holy mystery which surrounds the records of it precludes the possibility of our giving an exact description of what occurred. That it did occur is amply assured by its fruits in transforming a beaten little band of disciples, most of whom had run away after the arrest of Jesus in Gethsemane, into flaming witnesses for their Master. It was in this resurrection faith that the church was born and by it has been sustained to the present time.

There are skeptics who deny the objective occurrence of the Resurrection and make of it only a psychological event in which a new spirit possessed the disciples. But must we not say that this new spirit in them was the work of the Holy Spirit? We need not sharply distinguish between the living Christ and the Holy Spirit, for both are disclosures of the one God present in our daily lives. This continuing presence is sufficient evidence of fulfillment of the promise, "Lo, I am with you always."

Our knowledge of the Resurrection through a blend of external evidence and inner experience is typical of all religious knowledge. There are many "pathways to the reality of God," the title of an important book a generation ago by the Quaker philosopher Rufus M. Jones. There is the marvelous orderliness of nature which makes science possible. There is a world of beauty, which is best explained as the work of a beauty-loving Creator. There are evidences of progress in biological evolution and in human history which suggest a guiding divine purpose. To many minds, including mine, the Hebrew-Christian heritage as recorded in the Bible and coming to its supreme climax in the life, the ministry, and the cross of Jesus gives warmth

93

and meaning to these other evidences. And to all of these must be added the practical effects of religious faith in the lives of those who hold it seriously. Yet still it must be said that all these evidences fall short of proof.

At this point it is one's own inner experience that tips the scales of decision. It is a mistake to rely on what is often termed blind faith, though this might better be called credulity. Christian faith is not belief in the absurd; it is commitment in trust to what one's living experience validates. The "will to believe" of which another famous philosopher, William James, wrote so persuasively is not wishful thinking; it is decision based on the convergence of external evidence with the intuitions of the soul.

So let us not try to "prove" the Resurrection, or to say just what may have happened in it. But let us rest upon it in faith and hope, and know that because of it the living Christ is with us, right here, right now.

Lord Christ, help me to walk with you in daily companionship, to be guided, quickened, empowered by your presence. Amen.

23. Pentecost

When the day of Pentecost had come, they were all together in one place. . . .

(Acts 2:1 ff.)

The little shattered band, their leader lost,
Had found new hope on that first Easter day,
And so they met to wait at Pentecost;
The Spirit of truth would come—they had heard
    him say.

The miracle was wrought with tongues of flame,
A rushing mighty wind, strange speech, and then
The company was quickened. The Spirit came
And in this power the people were new men.

They shared with each as any one had need;
Partook of food with glad and generous hearts;
They witnessed to their faith and bade men heed
The glad, good news of what God's love imparts.

The Church was born. We owe an awesome debt.
Come, Holy Spirit, now—lest we forget.

It is a pity that Pentecost is not more widely
observed in the American churches. It is observed in England as Whitsunday, though perhaps more as a holiday than a holy day. In this
country it usually receives slight mention, if any,
and when the seventh Sunday after Easter coin-
cides with Mother's Day, as it does occasionally,
it is the latter that is celebrated.

Yet Pentecost is the birthday of the church.
It is, of course, possible to trace the origin of
the church back to the Old Testament covenant,
or in the New Testament to the ministry of
Jesus. Yet as a body of Christians knit together
with a settled purpose, the church begins with

the coming of the Holy Spirit at Pentecost, and we ought to observe this day with a holy joy.

What the church of today needs most for its renewal is a new Pentecost. This does not mean that there can be any exact repetition of the events of that day long ago so vividly described in the second chapter of Acts. Yet a number of things about it suggest directions for our time.

The disciples were together and waiting with expectancy. Millions of Christians throughout the world assemble for worship every Sunday, but too often neither minister nor congregation expects much to happen, and not much does.

The Spirit came in continuity with the past but with renewal of power in a new situation. Pentecost, which had originally been a Canaanite harvest festival, was a Jewish holy day observed fifty days after the Passover. Most if not all of those assembled were Jews, though from various parts of the Eastern world, and it was natural enough that they should come together to observe this day within their tradition. It was to this company and the bystanders that Peter preached his great sermon which centered in the life, the ministry, the death, and the resurrection of Jesus. From that day on, Christ's followers were to find in Pentecost a radically new meaning.

The Spirit came with power and quickened the disciples to a new joy. The symbolism of "the rush of a mighty wind" and "tongues as

96

of fire, distributed and resting on each one of them," suggests a vibrant enthusiasm, not in a flash-in-the-pan sense but in the root meaning of the word enthusiasm, which is "God within." Were we to feel a more vivid sense of the presence of God in our lives, we should probably not begin to speak in tongues, but all our speaking might be a more vital witness to our faith.

The Spirit came with a moral urgency that linked holiness with both fellowship and service. The last part of the chapter is, perhaps, even more of a miracle than its beginning, for those who became Christ's followers shared their possessions with any in need and entered into a joyous fellowship of teaching, learning, eating, and worshiping together. With this witness in their living, no wonder that "the Lord added to their number day by day those who were being saved"! Let us ask these gifts for our time.

Come, Holy Spirit, come!
We do not ask for flaming tongues of fire,
Or tongues that speak beyond our wonted way,
But come thou to our lives, our souls inspire,
And breathe thy Spirit into every day.

Like those of old expectantly we wait.
The promised Helper came to them with power;
So in our time of turmoil, strife and hate
We claim again the promise for this hour.
Come, Holy Spirit, come!

24. Thanksgiving

Let the nations be glad and sing for joy,
  for thou dost judge the peoples with equity
  and guide the nations upon earth.
Let the peoples praise thee, O God;
  let all the peoples praise thee!
                                    (Ps. 67:4-5)

Father all bountiful, thee we adore,
Filling our treasure-house out of thy store.
By thee our years are blest; by thee we live.
Grateful, we take from thee all thou dost give.

Though darkness shrouds the lands, still shines
  thy light.
Mercies that flow from thee gladden our night.
Blessings of home and kin, friendship and health
Come from thy gracious hand in boundless wealth.

Father who givest all, to thee we bring
Tribute of grateful hearts, thy praises sing.
Help us to use thy gifts to spread thy peace;
Give us thy Spirit, Lord, our love increase.

Thanksgiving Day is in reality a national rather than a Christian observance. Other countries observe it at different times, if at all, and in America it means as much to devout Jews as to Christians. Some of the most moving and worshipful corporate Thanksgiving services I have experienced were not only ecumenical but interfaith. However, it seems appropriate to include some words about this day among the great days of the Christian year, for it ought to be a special time of thanksgiving to God for grace abounding in a multitude of ways, material and spiritual, national and personal.

As for the circumstances of the writing of this poem, the friend who has shared my home for the past twenty-five years is a musician, as I am not, and she suggested that I write something which might be sung to the tune of "The Old Refrain." These lines are the result. The music cannot be reproduced here, but the reader is invited to try it for himself. The lovely cadences of "The Old Refrain" call to mind Fritz Kreisler, who played it so often, and all that he did to enrich life by his violin. Not for material abundance only, but also for grace abounding in art and manifold gifts of the spirit, we have reason in our thanksgiving to rejoice.

Yet these are dark days. As I write, the war goes on in Vietnam; racial tensions continue; the crime rate mounts; and dangerous drugs are destroying lives. There is a deep student unrest on many campuses. Moral codes of long standing are being widely flouted, and in the face of much talk about "law and order" not much of it seems to be emerging. In spite of great material abundance and tables laden with Thanksgiving viands for some, many others dwell in urban ghettos and pockets of rural poverty in our fair land. Around the world it

99

is deprivation rather than opulence that prevails. Can Christians really be thankful in such circumstances?

Not, certainly, in the spirit of the Pharisee who thanks God that he is not as other men are, whether in one's outward or his inner condition. The only kind of thanksgiving that rings true at this season is that which is offered in humility, in outgoing concern for others, and in the willingness to share God's good gifts.

Yet there are very precious things for which to give thanks that no darkness of the times can cancel out. Among them are the love of family and friends, a country dedicated to freedom and justice, the spiritual freedom to press toward the higher values, the enduring goodness of God's love. We do well to remember that this is not the first dark day in history, and that when the founding fathers of this nation were faced with what seemed to be insurmountable problems, they still were able to praise God for his goodness and press forward.

So from full hearts warm with gratitude let us give thanks! And with the psalmist let us say:

> Bless the Lord, O my soul;
> and all that is within me,
>   bless his holy name!
> Bless the Lord, O my soul,
>   and forget not all his benefits.
>
> (Ps. 103:1-2)

They Live Again

25. Eternal Tribute

Jesus said, . . . "She has done a beautiful thing to me. . . . She has done what she could; she has anointed my body beforehand for burying. And truly, I say to you, wherever the gospel is preached in the whole world, what she has done will be told in memory of her."

(Mark 14:6-9)

"She has done what she could," the Master spoke;
"In memory of her the story shall be told
Through all the world. Wherever human folk
Shall hear me and be gathered to my fold
There shall her loving deed make men's hearts
*   glad."*
And what was this that gained so high reward?
A simple thing but costing all she had—
An alabaster love-gift for her Lord.

And one I knew who in her time and place,
Like Mary, brought her gift of love, her all.
The fragrance of her life is rich with grace;
It wakes my soul to hear the Master's call.
I thank thee, Lord, my life touched one so good,
So worthy of thy praise, "She has done what she
*   could."*

We come now to a different theme from the preceding. From time to time as friends I loved have died, I have written a memorial poem. It was usually in the form of a sonnet, for this carries within its designated structure a dignity and depth which in my judgment is not quite native to any other verse form.

I have hesitated to include these memorial poems, for obviously in most cases the readers will not have been acquainted with the persons about and to whom they were written. Yet I have decided to do so for two reasons. One is that these persons have their counterparts in many places, and what is said may suggest to the reader someone from his own circle of friends. The second reason is that in every case these persons were Christians who carried eternity in the nature of their living as well as in their dying. Whatever the critics may say, being a Christian *does* make a difference!

In the first section of the book tribute was paid to a long line of country ministers, some of whom have left me a lasting heritage. I am grateful to God for what they contributed to my growing years and early adulthood. The poem included under the title "Benediction" states my feeling about several of them, though it would be unrealistic to suggest that this states my judgment of all of them.

Yet the minister is only one part of the parsonage family. The poem which introduces the present section was written about a minister's wife in whose home I often found encouragement and an undergirding friendship. She is long since gone, but her two daughters, both of whom chose professions in Christian work, remain my good friends over the years.

This friend of whom the poem speaks was locally beloved but not widely known, an unpretentious but devoted Christian. She was active in the church in whatever capacity the occasion called for. Yet in retrospect it was not her leadership, but her down-to-earth goodness that stands out. She did what she could, and did not seem to worry that her role was not cast for doing more.

Let these words then speak for the woman, whether minister's wife, layman's wife, or single woman, who in her own time and place does what she can and leaves the world enriched by the fragrance of Christian fidelity and love.

Lord, I thank thee that thou hast blest my life with grace abounding in so many folk of humble goodness. May their memory like their presence draw me closer to thee and make me more faithful. Amen.

26. To One Who Spent Herself Early

O death, where is thy victory?
(I Cor. 15:55a)

To live but half the mortal span of years
And pass betimes to realms beyond the light,

105

Is this not folly, tragic waste? Can tears
Give way to clearness lighting up the night?

To live with courage, battling heavy odds,
To smooth with vibrant wit the roughened ways,
To heal with skill, with tender touch, God's
Suffering ones—this is to live great days!

As once the body of a strong young Jew
Was broken early, died upon a cross
That all God's sons might live, so gave she too
Her strength. Call not such giving loss;
For by her body broken for God's poor
Souls are made rich, God's way of love proved
    sure.

This is in memory of the daughter of a family knit to me by close ties—a minister's family, though not that of the preceding meditation. Her father was the Keeseville pastor during my high school days, a person of unusual intellectual ability who did much to shape my religious thinking. When many years later my *Understanding the Christian Faith* was published, I dedicated it to him with the words "lifelong pastor, teacher, and friend, who in retirement continues to think and to blaze new trails." He has since gone to heaven, perhaps there to continue this process.

But the poem is of Charis, not her father. Through the years I watched her grow from a small child with surgical operations on her dolls to a very efficient and selfless physician, and then on to her too early death. It is unusual for a small child to know what he wants to do when he grows up and to stay with it. Yet from the time I first knew her, when she was about five, she wanted to be a doctor. Her parents encouraged but did not dominate her in this choice. It was an economic struggle both for her and them to put her through college and medical school at a time when preacher's salaries were much less than today, and her father was not appointed to large churches, but it was done.

Desiring to serve where the need was great, Charis took an appointment to a hospital in Puerto Rico, and as a skilled obstetrician brought hundreds of little brown babies into the world. She never spared herself, saying jocularly about the twenty-four–hour work periods she sometimes had that she was "tough and durable." Yet by some unknown cause probably intensified by overstrain, cancer developed in her sturdy body during her mid-thirties, and not long after that she was gone.

Why was a person so useful and needed taken away so soon? This is the query of the ages, both a cry of the heart and a perplexity of the mind. I shall not attempt to answer it, save to say that we do not really answer it by

107

the old cliché, "It was the will of God." God wills his human children to have health and happiness, with many years of service to one another. The healing miracles of Jesus, far exceeding in number all others that are recorded, are sufficient evidence of this. We had better say that there are certain basic laws of nature within our bodies; they operate impersonally, but within limits can be utilized by the physician's skill to heal. Beyond these limits, death at whatever time it comes is the destiny of us all.

In Ecclesiasticus, an excellent book of wisdom literature which failed to get into the Old Testament canon but which is found in the Apocrypha, there is a fine tribute to physicians. Let me quote part of it now as a tribute to Charis and her kind.

My son, in thy sickness be not negligent;
But pray unto the Lord, and he shall heal thee.
Put away wrong doing, and order thine hands
    aright,
And cleanse thy heart from all manner of sin. . . .
Then give place to the physician, for verily the
    Lord hath created him;
And let him not go from thee, for thou hast need
    of him.
There is a time when in their very hands is the
    issue for good.
For they also shall beseech the Lord,

That he may prosper them in giving relief and
in healing for the maintenance of life.
(Ecclus. 38:9-14)

Lord, we see as in a mirror dimly. Yet there is
a clear light in the living of one who for others
strongly lives and nobly dies. We thank thee that
such lives have touched ours and blest us. Amen.

27. Postlude

Peace I leave with you; my peace I give to you;
not as the world gives do I give to you. Let not
your hearts be troubled, neither let them be afraid.
(John 14:27)

When fields were white last Christmas time
I went to see my friend.
With clear white victory she smiled;
Serene, she faced the end.
Today the fields are white again—
I cannot hear her voice:
Yet round me still her radiance glows
And still I can rejoice.

They gave me of her earthly store
The Bible that she used.
Well worn it is, with many a mark
Of thoughts on which she mused.
She found in it the quickening words
That made her spirit strong.

109

In Christ she lived: she lives in death—
A never-dying song.

This bit of verse was written about an older woman friend who manifested to an unusual degree the "holy living" and "holy dying" about which Jeremy Taylor wrote some three centuries ago. She was for many years the competent editor of the county newspaper, which often printed historical articles written by my father. However, what drew us together was her love of the church and especially her vital interest in foreign missions. Earlier, so I have been told, she was a somewhat casual Christian until her minister (Charis' father) kindled in her that which made her a vibrant, though unpretentious, witness to Christ in all her living.

She never married. In earlier days she might have been termed a spinster, or more colloquially "an old maid." Fortunately, one does not now hear these terms very often, and I never heard them applied to her. However, it is still not unusual to find the older unmarried woman viewed with pity, if not with some suspicion of abnormal traits. To answer this charge let me quote from Margot Benary-Isbert's delightful book, *These Vintage Years:* "The legendary frustrated spinster seems to be extinct or to have survived only as a rare residue. Most of the unmarried elderly women I know have aged gracefully. They are well adjusted, calm, serene,

110

and content with their lives. After retirement they keep busy and useful with their multitude of interests and abilities." [6]

This accords with my observation. However, our present concern is not to argue this point, but to ask how death can be confronted with such serenity that one can talk freely about it with no trace of fear or morbidness and meet it without a quiver. This my friend did.

Perhaps the surest evidence of one's personality—what one is at the center of existence—is one's attitude toward death. It does not need to be talked about frequently to be evident. While most people shrink with dread from the necessity of dying, others court it too eagerly with the hope of escaping life's troubles. Hamlet's "To be, or not to be" is an eternal, even if seldom stated, question. Yet there are others who view death as within the providence of God, and the next step in life's many adventures. To these persons death like life is the gift of God, to be entered into with challenge and expectancy when the summons comes.

Said John Wesley of the persons who had found Christ through the early Methodist societies, "Our people die well." I doubt that the only people who "die well" are Christians. Yet I am sure that the Christian gospel, taken seriously, makes a great difference. In part this

[6] (Nashville: Abingdon Press, 1968), p. 61.

is due to the Christian faith in life after death, often questioned but still remaining as a basic note in our Christian heritage. Yet eternal life begins here on earth, and it is what the good news of God does to life on this side of death that robs death of its terrors. For living or dying, "the peace of God which passes all understanding" is available for our taking.

Lord of heaven and earth, save us from the fear of dying and from idle lamentation when those we love are taken from us. Let our grief be transfigured by faith, and whatever the issues of life, help us to face forward. Amen.

28. The Upward Path

The steps of a good man are ordered by the Lord: and he delighteth in his way. Though he fall, he shall not be utterly cast down: for the Lord upholdeth him with his hand.

(Ps. 37:23-24 KJV)

Beloved friend and valiant soul he is,
In whom the light divine is strong and clear:
For kindliness and faith undimmed are his
To serve in love and greet the dawn with cheer.

To know him was to feel his gentle grace;
His spirit triumphed over flesh and pain.
It gave new peace to look upon his face,
To feel his handclasp, strong amid the strain.

112

Like beacon shining high above our night
To lead men toward the everlasting Day,
So gleams his spirit with celestial light
To guide his fellow travelers in the way.

We follow then the upward path he trod.
To know such life was good. We thank thee,
God.

In the three preceding meditations we have paid tribute to laywomen, differing from one another in temperament and vocation but united in fidelity to Christ and his work within our world. We look now at the contribution of a layman—not an outstanding layman as this term is commonly used, but a good man and a good Christian. He served on no major boards or commissions; his name will not go down to posterity in the annals of the church. He is remembered, I am sure, by the older members of his local church where he served faithfully, but I doubt that the younger half of its membership would recognize his name if it were spoken.

Why then include this tribute? For two reasons: first, because he *was* a good man and a good Christian; second, because it is men like him that make up the supporting bulwark of our churches. Much is being said today, and often deservedly, about the conservatism of the laity which stands in the way of forward movements in the direction of needed social action. Much less is said of those sturdy laymen with-

113

out whose support, not only financial but moral and spiritual, the church would go on the rocks as a stable institution helping to hold society together. Both elements are needed—both social change and stability amid the change.

A further word may be said about this particular layman. When his widow arranged for his memorial service after they had together fought a long and valiant fight against terminal cancer, she entitled it, "The Upward Trail: A Service of Loving and Joyous Commemoration." This is the mood a memorial service ought to have, not one of gloom but of grateful and joyous appreciation, and I was glad to contribute my words as a part of it. I believe them to be a true description, for within a limited circle and without the world's acclaim the spirit of this man cast its light steadily forward on the upward path. And can any of us do more?

"The steps of a good man are ordered by the Lord," says the psalmist. In the apocryphal book entitled the Wisdom of Solomon, to which reference was made earlier when we found its author citing the beauty of nature as a witness to its Creator against all false gods, there are some great words about the durability of virtue. They have the ring of triumph as well as tribute.

For in the memory of virtue is immortality:
Because it is recognised both before God and before men.

When it is present, men imitate it;
And they long after it when it is departed:
And throughout all time it marcheth crowned in
 triumph,
Victorious in the strife for the prizes that are
 undefiled. (4:1-2)

With that kind of victory, there is no need of
the plaudits of the world.

Save us, O God, from seeking the prizes that
are transient when those that endure are ours for
the taking. Make firm our steps in the way thou
hast set before us, and thy favor shall be our sufficient reward. Amen.

29. To a Gentle Soul of Valiant Strength

His master said to him, "Well done, good and
faithful servant; you have been faithful over a
little, I will set you over much; enter into the joy
of your master."

(Matt. 25:23)

He was a gentle soul, of valiant strength,
In him was life forever young and strong:
Around the world men loved him, for the
 length
Of shadow that he cast was straight and long.

115

In kindliness and firm fidelity
He stirred the deeps within each answering
*   soul.*
The Christian faith and deeds, he saw, must be
Knit into one to make of life a whole.

The new year comes—the old must have an
*   end—*
And many a wish is spoken, kind and true.
So, forward turns the spirit of our friend
To work with God in fields of service new.

As he sets forth upon this last great quest
We joy with him, adventure at its best!

This is a memorial tribute to another layman, but unlike the previous one, a man widely known with many honors. He was a person of much ability, wide education, and wisdom-generating experience, which he used in the service of God and his fellowmen. He served for many years with the YMCA in Japan, where he received an award from the emperor for outstanding contributions. Returning to this country, he held an important post in social and religious research, directing in India, China, and Japan studies which were incorporated in the Laymen's Foreign Missions Inquiry of 1931. When the Japanese of the West Coast were interned during the Second World War, he fought valiantly for justice in their behalf.

It was in connection with the Pacific School of Religion that I came to know him well, though I was familiar with his name before coming to it. He was long the president of its Board of Trustees and was its acting president in interim periods. The great memorial window in its Chapel of the Great Commission is named in his honor. In one of his later years he received the distinguished service award granted by his city to its most outstanding and useful citizen.

Here apparently was a man who "had everything," for in addition to such honors he had money enough for comfortable living, a fine home with a loving and loyal family, and a wealth of friends. Not only his achievements but his gracious and gentle spirit won them to him. To quote once more from the Wisdom of Solomon, he was "victorious in the strife for the prizes that are undefiled" (4:2). I believe he was a happy man; at least, in a quiet way he always gave this impression.

Two questions may arise. The first is whether it is possible to be thus richly blest and still remain a humble Christian seeking neither power nor status for oneself. The answer is yes. It was true of this man; it is true repeatedly, though not often enough. Perhaps I have been unusually fortunate in knowing a considerable number of people in whom such simple goodness outshone any honors the world might give them, but I am sure there are more of them than the cynics are in the habit of saying.

117

The second question is in a different area, and perhaps more difficult. Does God prize such a person more highly than the rest of us? Certainly God must rejoice in such able and faithful service. God's "Well done, good and faithful servant" is the highest reward anyone can have, and if earthly honors should come to us, we do well to receive them not only graciously but also gratefully as the gift of God. Yet our faith in the love of God tells us that "God shows no partiality" (Acts 10:34). If this be true, the forgotten, homeless waif, or the offender against society, or the respectable but self-willed sinner is as precious to God as any of his saints. Perhaps God alone can have such impartial and all-encompassing vision, but we do well to try to emulate it.

We thank thee, God, for grace abounding to us through those persons in whom we see manifest the fruits of thy Spirit. We too would be gentle souls of valiant strength, made gentle and strong by thee. Amen.

30. To a Christian Saint

Let your light so shine before men, that they may see your good works and give glory to your Father who is in heaven.

(Matt. 5:16)

We honor one in whom there was no guile,
A Christian saint, kind, stalwart, great of heart
It was his life to walk the second mile;
In many a noble work he took his part
And asked no recompense or high acclaim.
His soul reached out to lands beyond the sun.
In warmth of friendly welcome in Christ's name
His heart and hand were open. Every one
Of high or low estate could call him friend.
And then as passed the old year to the new,
For us came grief. For him life has no end,
And Heaven is richer for this soul so true.
We thank thee, Lord, that such a man as he
Has dwelt with us, and now shall live with thee.

The term "Christian saint" ought not to be used lightly. There are not many persons to whom it properly applies, and it should not be bandied about without due discrimination. Yet there *are* Christian saints in our time, Protestant as well as Catholic, marked by the kind of life they manifest and not by the official canonization of the church.

This poem pays tribute to one of them, a minister for thirty years in a large suburban church. The motto of his life was Peter's word in regard to Jesus, "He went about doing good" (Acts 10:38). At his memorial service an unusual thing occurred. So down to earth was he in his goodness, so widely beloved and appreciated, that when his parishioners and many others met in a packed church to pay him trib-

119

ute there was laughter—natural, wholesome laughter—at some witticism about his extraordinary "second mile" activities.

There is not space to enumerate them all, but some samples will suffice. As a young man just out of college he spent two years in India, and for the rest of his life he and his wife gave a generous share of their income to maintain one student missionary after another at the college where he had taught. To many causes they gave with an outgoing generosity, not of money only but of costly time and effort. No one knows how many hundreds of boxes of food and clothing he personally packed and sent to deprived or displaced persons abroad. Their home was a haven for overseas travelers on God's business, who sometimes came and went at ungodly hours, and I recall his driving the sixty miles to and from the airport to pick up one of them at 4 A.M. It was through such contacts that he introduced a good many distinguished leaders to the Berkeley community. Yet one did not need to be a distinguished person to receive the hospitality of this home, for any sick or lonely person without other adequate provision would find a haven there.

We are called by our gospel to be agents of reconciliation. He was a lifelong member of the Fellowship of Reconciliation, and thus a Christian pacifist. Yet in a wider sense his more than forty years in the ministry were a lifelong mission of reconciliation—the bringing of men to God and the healing of earth's wounds, both physical and spiritual. I doubt that any who knew him will doubt the accuracy of the statement that here was "one in whom there was no guile, a Christian saint." Thank God for such as he in our troubled, strife-torn world!

This completes the roll call of those to whom I have paid memorial tributes, except for some poems which have appeared in other books. The persons presented have been both men and women, older and younger, some unknown save in a limited circle and some widely known and honored. I have inserted no names, for God knows them all, their friends will recognize them, and other readers may find what has been said suggesting persons of their own acquaintance. Differing as they do, they still have one thing in common—they were devoted Christians in whom the divine light shone.

Says John's Gospel of the life which was the light of men, "The light shines in the darkness, and the darkness has not overcome it" (1:5). As long as this light continues to shine in persons like these, we need not despair of our times, of the church, or of God's eternal presence.

We thank thee, God, for grace abounding in such lives. Amen.

121

*In Quest
of a Better
Society*

31. Holy Flame

And I heard the voice of the Lord saying, "Whom
shall I send, and who will go for us?" Then I
said, "Here I am! Send me."

(Isa. 6:8)

Isaiah mourned the passing of the king,
And to the temple came to muse and pray.
Dark was the kingdom's future on that day,
Beset with greed and every evil thing.
No spokesman of the Lord was there to sting
The conscience of the mob, or lead the way
To gallant victories in Jehovah's fray
With sin and strife, with self and suffering.

God gave Isaiah then the vision high;
His unclean lips were purged with sacred fire.
Out of the smoke a Voice in challenge came;
Unhesitant, he answered, Here am I.
. Again the days are dark, the outlook dire;
Lord, touch Thy prophets now with holy flame.

In the previous sections the poems have
spoken of beauty, peace, and the goodness of
God's world through which he speaks a reas-
suring Word. This is the dominant note of unspoiled nature. Yet there are ugly and destructive elements, even in the natural order, which
have not yet been subdued to human good. The

ancient edict to "fill the earth and subdue it" (Gen. 1:28) still stands—a suggestion of an unfinished and continuing creation in which God calls his servants to be co-creators. Still more clearly is this true of the enormous amount of sin and suffering in the world of human affairs.

The inclusion of this poem is a departure from my usual procedure of omitting those previously published in books now in print, for it is the title poem of my first volume of verse issued back in the 1930's, and it appears also in *Be Still and Know.* I place it here for two reasons. One is that it is the first serious poem I ever wrote, and hence something like a first baby! But a more important reason is its relevance to the present in spite of having been written many years ago during the days of the Great Depression.

In some respects the situation now is very different, for in spite of the bitter poverty of some, and far too many, there are wages, salaries, and an abundance of material goods undreamed of then. Yet these too are dark days, perhaps in some respects darker. I am not one to bewail the present and yearn for "the good old days," for within my memory I have seen great advances, not only in the economic foundations of life but also in the conquest of disease, in the spread of educational opportunities, in provision for help through many agencies of social

126

welfare, in civil rights legislation, and in progress toward racial justice and international order, in spite of much more to be done in these fields. Yet without undue optimism or pessimism it is still necessary to say, "Again the days are dark, the outlook dire," and to call upon God to raise up prophets for our time.

The poem was written in the era of the social gospel, which was held to with courage and conviction and proclaimed valiantly from pulpits, though by a minority of Christian leaders. It had its prophets, among them such men as Ernest Fremont Tittle, who was my pastor for a decade. Some say that such men were too optimistic and had too little awareness of the need to combat the great power structures of society, though this judgment does not accord with my recollection. In any case, the social gospel fell into disfavor as the currents of religious thought moved away from the liberal theology which it accompanied into neo-orthodoxy. Now it appears to be returning, not usually under this name but in connection with the renewal of the church and the need to make Christianity relevant to the needs of the secular world.

It is not the name but the deeds and their foundations which matter. Both the Old Testament prophets and the ministry and words of Jesus call us to the service of mankind and the

127

quest for a better world. To this quest this cycle of poems is devoted.

Lord God of our fathers and of every age, open our eyes to the needs of a suffering world. Banish our complacency; quicken our minds to discern our duty; make strong our spirits to speak and to act in the service of the people. In thee is our trust. Amen.

32. The Treaty

Repay no one evil for evil, but take thought for what is noble in the sight of all. If possible, so far as it depends upon you, live peaceably with all. . . . Do not be overcome by evil, but overcome evil with good.

(Rom. 12:17-18, 21)

Beneath a stately elm sat Taminen.
The Indians' council fires burned cheerily.
All Nature was aglow—it was autumn then—
The air was vibrant with expectancy.

"He lingers long," a swarthy chieftain spoke.
"He bade us come all weaponless, and wait.
Is he too false? Again shall white man's smoke
Lay waste our fields and homes? Will hate breed hate?"

"Look there—a barge!" cried one. "He comes! he comes!

I see his banner flying at the mast!"
"I trust him not. Mark well my word, our homes
Will lie in ashes ere this moon be past!"

Then up rose Taminen, and spoke. "Be still.
Each footprint in the wood, each sign I know.
I read men too, and these come not to kill.
They are our friends. Arise and greet them so!"

Some shook their heads and seemed not to accord
But all arose and spoke their fear no more.
They made their way across the leaf-strewn
*   sward*
To where the English craft drew near to shore.

Beside the helmsman stood the Governor
In simple dignity, not arrogant nor meek.
Chief Taminen put on his chaplet as for war
And bade the Quaker chieftain land and speak.

"We come in love," said Penn. "We come un-
*   armed,*
And He who rules the heavens and the earth
Knows well our thought. No brother shall be
*   harmed:*
Our bulwarks shall be fellowship and mirth.

"We ask no oath, no hostage. Plighted word
Shall be our surety, for each man is brother.
Draw near, my friends! As many as have heard
And give assent, pledge fealty each to other!"

They pledged, and vowed the bond should be
*   forever;*
Their sons should keep it stainless, fair and pure.
They said the treaty should be broken never
While rivers run, while moon and stars endure.

129

Their shouts rang out to meet the skies above;
The very trees with crimson joy were filled.
They dwelt in peace, secure in bonds of love.
The pledge was kept: no brother's blood was
spilled.

This is one of my few narrative poems. It is scarcely an epic, but its theme, rooted in history, does have an epic grandeur. In 1681 King Charles II of England gave to the Quaker William Penn some 45,000 square miles of land in America in return for a debt owed to Penn's father. Penn asked for settlers to form a colony where there would be freedom of religion and government for the good of all, urging especially his fellow Quakers to join him. On arrival he bought land from the Indians and made a peace treaty with them in which both sides agreed that there should be no bloodshed between them "while rivers run, while moon and stars endure." The treaty held, and both the Indians and the settlers lived in peace and mutual security throughout the entire history of the colony.

Fantastic? So it may seem in view of today's clashes between opposing groups which so easily become war, and then more war until great numbers of persons on both sides are killed and all humanity is jeopardized. Many will say that Penn's way of dealing with the Indians, like the Quaker nonviolence of today, makes a pretty story but will not work amid the complexities
130

of today's world. Yet within the twentieth century it worked with Gandhi to secure India's independence from what was the mightiest empire of the Western world. It might work again if given a chance, not with a supine surrender to evil forces but in a genuine spirit of reconciliation.

I went through the period of the First World War without any important deviation from conventional American thinking, justifying our intervention, thinking the Germans wholly the cause of the war, deploring its destruction, but believing there was no alternative. Like others I rejoiced with a frenzy of delight when we heard that the armistice had been signed. I was studying at Boston University at the time, and I shall never forget the enthusiasm with which we raced across the city to Fanueil Hall to celebrate the end of this and supposedly all wars. At that time a pacifist position that would oppose all war on grounds of Christian conscience did not occur to me.

It was not until the summer of 1924, when I went to Europe with the Sherwood Eddy party, that I began seriously to consider this position. We heard statesmen of many countries speak, making clear the broader causes of the recent war and showing that the blame could not all be laid on Germany. I became acquainted with some outstanding American pacifists, and their position made sense. As a result I joined the

Fellowship of Reconciliation, of which I have remained a member to the present.

During the Korean War I offered to withdraw from the FOR, for I had come to believe that there were occasions when international police action under the United Nations might be justified. Its leaders advised me to continue, and I have done so, for I cannot in Christian conscience sanction the use of military force by one nation against another with all the horrible destructiveness which war entails. The Vietnam War is, I believe, a moral and social disaster for both the Vietnamese and the American people, and could not be otherwise under the conditions of modern warfare.

So that treaty of peace from long ago between William Penn and Chief Taminen is more than a curious tale. It reflects deep wisdom for our time and for every time of human conflict. Paul's dictum which reflects the mind of Jesus, "Do not be overcome by evil, but overcome evil with good," is not only right but realistic in the fullest sense. The sooner we begin to apply it, the better for our nation and for the world.

Lord God of hosts, thou whose reign is over all the nations, give peace in our time. Help us to obey thy call to concern and service toward all men, and in thy ways of righteousness to find our security and strength. Amen.

33. The Innocents

It is not the will of my Father who is in heaven
that one of these little ones should perish.

(Matt. 18:14)

"Lord, when did we see thee hungry or thirsty or
a stranger or naked or sick or in prison, and did
not minister to thee?" Then he will answer them,
"Truly, I say to you, as you did it not to one of
the least of these, you did it not to me."

(Matt. 25:44-45)

In bygone days of Herod the king—
A time of which we love to sing—
In Bethlehem was born a boy
Whose birth we celebrate with joy.

And sing we must, for with Him arose
New hope for man, as the Christian knows,
And ancient ways of guilt and sin
Are vanquished as He enters in.

But what of the innocents that died,
The babes that were killed as Herod's pride
And savage lust for acclaim and power
Make dark the shadows of that hour?

And what of the innocents today
Whom we with deadly fire bombs slay,
Who die from lack of daily rice,
A pitiful, wordless sacrifice?

Lest we like Herod destroy the weak
Thy cleansing grace, O Lord, we seek.

From callous sin our souls set free,
O Christ, the man of Galilee.

This poem was written much more recently
than the preceding one. It was prompted chiefly
by a soul-sickening knowledge of the suffering
of the innocents in Vietnam—little children,
their mothers, and their aged grandparents
caught in the crossfires of a war they did not
make and cannot understand. Dying, maimed,
and homeless by the thousands, these innocent
civilians are a "pitiful, wordless sacrifice" on the
altar of political dispute and fumbling on the
part of major powers. Not yet have the nations
learned that the old, bloody pathway of war
and its horrible destruction of life and the resources for living must give way to other modes
of settlement.

Nor is the suffering of the innocents limited to
Vietnam. As these words are written, one hears
of starving children dying daily by the hundreds
in Biafra. In many parts of the world there is
hunger, malnutrition, and needless disease. In
our own land there are hungry people, and
many live in substandard, rat-infested ghettos
where infant mortality is high.

It is well that these matters have become political issues, for the conscience of America
ought not to be at ease before such circumstances. It is important to have the right leaders.

Yet in a democracy leaders do what they believe the citizens demand, and the guilt for these situations must be shared by all who have been callous to our Lord's injunctions to compassionate service. And, if we are honest with ourselves, that means most of us!

We are not told much about the reaction to Herod's slaying of the male babies, although there is a touching reference to "wailing and loud lamentation, Rachel weeping for her children," and refusing to be consoled because they were no more (Matt. 2:18). In the book of Lamentations, which tells of the suffering of the people after Jerusalem had fallen to its conquerors, the description is more extended and poignant, and it comes to focus in the words, "Is it nothing to you, all you who pass by?"

The world has had some twenty-five centuries to answer this cry, and nearly twenty since the cruelty of Herod. Yet still the suffering of the innocents continues, and one of the gravest elements is the indifference and complacency of comfortable Christians. Perhaps our Lord is saying to us today, "Is it nothing to you, all you who pass by?" If so, let us open our ears and our hearts to hear him and our hands and our wills to act.

Forgive us, Lord, and grant us the grace of compassion. Amen.

135

34. For Conscience

And when they had brought them, they set them before the council. And the high priest questioned them, saying, "We strictly charged you not to teach in this name, yet here you have filled Jerusalem with your teaching and you intend to bring this man's blood upon us." But Peter and the apostles answered, "We must obey God rather than men."

(Acts 5:27-29)

> For conscience Socrates
> Taught Athens' youth, and did not please
> The guardians of the state. He drank
> The fatal cup, nor from it shrank.
>
> For conscience Jesus too
> Withstood the ruling powers to do
> In love his Father's will. He died
> With thieves, in triumph crucified.
>
> For conscience men today,
> Combating war's barbaric sway,
> Resist the state. They will not kill.
> Is God or man the higher will?

These words deal with one of the most difficult of all human decisions—the rightness or wrongness of resistance to the state by the conscientious objector to war. It is a concrete case of the wider issue of whether civil disobedience is ever justified. It is certain that the Christian church was born in an atmosphere of civil disobedience, of which the words quoted from the book of Acts are but one instance of defiance of the ruling powers in order to proclaim the gospel. It is clear that the total impact of Jesus' teaching was in the direction of love, brotherhood and building, not destruction, and that the use of the "whip of small cords" in the temple incident has no connection whatever with the atrocities of every war. Still, the issue remains a cloudy one.

The complexity of the matter centers in the thin line between the wars of aggression and of defense, in the difficulty of weighing the horrors of war against possible need to protect the defenseless, in the fact that some situations seem to present no viable alternatives. Add to these the social stigma and possible imprisonment of one who refuses military service, and the morally sensitive but still immature young man is faced with one of the most difficult decisions any person must make.

For those who felt in the Second World War that their allegiance to God ruled out participation in war, there were Civilian Public Service camps. I visited some of these, and while the camps did not seem very fruitful, I found among the young men in them great strength of character and very little that looked like draft-dodging. Today there are no C.P.S. camps, and those with conscientious scruples on religious grounds are legally eligible for exemption with alternate service in other fields.

Yet a new phenomenon has arisen, related to the "just war" doctrine formulated by Augustine many centuries ago. Thousands who are not pacifists regarding all war are so convinced that the Vietnam War is unjust and immoral that they will not fight in it. Some of these have religious motives, others apparently do not. This has given rise to selective conscientious objection, and because this position is not recognized by law, to civil disobedience.

I believe that selective conscientious objection is here to stay, and where it is truly conscientious, it ought to be respected. Though I do not sanction draft evasion or violent defiance, when a young man has faced the whole matter in the depths of his being and is willing to accept the consequences, should not both the church and the law uphold him in it?

There is no single answer to this complex question, and not all Christians will agree. What we can do is to respect the positions of those who differ and to work mightily as far as we can for reconciliation and justice among the nations. Though most of the major decisions must be made by those in high places of authority, every person can do something. By one's voting, one's speaking, indeed, by the tenor of one's living, one can help to tip the scales for or against the occasions of war. And what we can do, we ought to do, by the help of God.

Make me a peacemaker, Lord, beginning where I am. Help me to bring thy word of reconciliation to our strife-torn world. Amen.

35. Black

And Peter opened his mouth and said: "Truly I perceive that God shows no partiality, but in every nation any one who fears him and does what is right is acceptable to him."

(Acts 10:34-35)

Snatched from the jungle, torn from his home,
Carried by white men over the foam,

Under the slave lash put to strange labor,
Welcome as servant, not friend or neighbor,

Freed from his serfdom by carnage and
   blood,
Lifted from bondage, raised from the mud,

Freedom—but was it? No liberty this,
Affronted with scorn, reviling and hiss,

Crucified daily, he suffers in shame,
Disdained by white brothers who bear Christ's
   name,

Singing, his spirit bursts from its thongs,
And rises to greatness, freed by its songs.

I believe I wrote these lines after listening to a concert by Roland Hayes, though it may

139

have been Marian Anderson. In any case, it was before the racial issue had surfaced as it has of late. After hesitating between discarding and rewriting it, I am leaving it as it is, for its basic theme has not changed with the passage of time.

The greatness of the Negro race does not lie wholly in its songs. It has produced great scientists, statesmen, authors, educators, preachers, and prophets. There is scarcely an important field of human endeavor in which important examples cannot be cited. It is well that Negroes of today have a fresh sense of the greatness of their heritage, whether in famous names or in the simple goodness of unknown but great souls.

Yet it remains true that the outstanding, distinctive gift of the Negro to America is in his spirituals. This is the only authentic and presumably lasting folk music we have. Compared with what today passes as folk music, crooned to electric guitars by long-haired youth, it is heaven-high. It voices the sorrows, the hopes, the great assurances of a people long deprived of their just rights, yet unwilling to surrender to despair because of their religious faith. It is no accident that such hymns as "Lord, I Want to Be a Christian in My Heart" and "Were You There When They Crucified My Lord?" have found an enduring place in our hearts and in our hymnals. Seldom is there an informal "sing" of any religious group that somebody does not start "We Are Climbing Jacob's Ladder." And "Let Us Break Bread Together on Our Knees" sounded an ecumenical note long before there was a movement by this name.

To say that the spirit of the black man is "freed by its songs" is, of course, not the whole story. Such spiritual freedom is no guarantee of being granted political or economic freedom. The long delay in "liberty and justice for all" has understandably bred bitterness and in some cases violence. Yet it was the spiritual urgency of a deep Christian faith that gave Martin Luther King, Jr., his "dream," and this must press on to fulfillment.

A major responsibility rests upon the churches in these matters. The report of the President's National Advisory Commission on Civil Disorders has made it unmistakably clear that white racism is a cancerous growth in our society, not limited to any single area. The civil rights legislation of recent years is a long step forward, but it must be implemented by changes in attitudes. As citizens and simply as intelligent human beings, we need to recognize the equal human dignity of persons of all races and stations in life. However, a special responsibility rests upon those who worship and profess allegiance to the God who "shows no partiality." He has made us all in his own spiritual image, and it is a basic blasphemy to fail to honor and serve him

141

by extending fellowship and the fruits of brotherhood to all.

We thank thee, God, for diversities of race and
color as of gifts among all thy children. Help us
to prize what thou hast given us, to honor what
we see in others, and to work together through
thy leading toward a world of freedom, equality,
and justice for all. Amen.

36. Walls

Behold, I have set before you an open door, which
no one is able to shut.

(Rev. 3:8)

Unbeautiful and cold, a prison wall
Sets bounds between two worlds. A guarded gate
Gave me ingress today. I glimpsed the fate
Of men—young men they were—who in some
*   brawl*
Had struck hot-browed, now "in for life," a pall
Across their years. In calculating hate
Some slew, and thought by death to vindicate
A rankling wound—the cause they scarce recall.

Well fed they are, and clothed; their ailments
*   tended;*
They play, and work, and live securely here.
I doubt not some I saw had suffered more
While hunger gnawed, before they had offended.

142

Then why that listless eye, face turned in fear?
Walls block the way. They see no open door.

This poem was written after a visit to a prison in upstate New York, some twenty-five miles from my old home. It is located in a small village surrounded by a pleasant countryside, and I am told that it was located there because the possibility of escape without detection is less in open country than in an urban situation with its many hiding places.

Adjacent to the prison is a hospital for the criminally insane. As far as I know, the conditions there, as in the prison, are humane. There is work therapy and an opportunity for reading and recreation, and the guards have few disturbances to cope with. Yet when they or the neighbors refer to this institution, it is commonly called "the bug house," and the patients or inmates in it "the bugs." Such unfortunate persons appear to have lost their personhood.

I do not wish to comment much on current penology. Yet in spite of the dark picture presented by life imprisonment, capital punishment is worse. It is a sub-Christian, subcivilized retaliatory system which has no discernible effect on the deterrence of crime and puts to death too many persons whose guilt has not been proved. Even were no innocent person ever its victim, it is rehabilitation, not retaliation by judicial

143

murder, which ought to be the goal of the punishment of offenders.

I suppose that until the Kingdom comes in our imperfect society, prisons will be necessary. What disturbs me most are not the walls described above but the walls which have so often brought these persons to committing offenses against society, and which confine many others. These are walls of poverty, with all its limiting circumstances; walls of prejudice whether racial, religious, or economic; walls of substandard education and early dropouts; walls of dismal and overcrowded housing and slum surroundings; walls of oversized families with neither material goods nor loving attention enough to go around; walls where alcohol and drunkenness do their disastrous work; walls of tension and bickering in both poor families and those of the well-to-do; walls of too great sternness without understanding; walls of too great leniency without discipline. Such walls, found throughout the land, are more confining than any prison.

But what of the open door? The words quoted from the book of Revelation were written by a political prisoner on the lonely island of Patmos, and the author represents the Spirit as speaking to the churches. They were written to tell those suffering for their faith under the persecutions of the Roman emperor Domitian that whatever happened to them, nothing could close the door to the encompassing love and power of God.

The message still stands. Plenty of things limit the capacity of a person to follow the patterns approved by the surrounding culture, and these tend to dull his religious sensitivity as well. Yet nothing can close the door to a better life in Christ if the message gets through. Evangelism is no easy matter in such circumstances. But when witness to the gospel is demonstrated by acts of loving concern and a resolute effort to lift the confining barriers, doors are opened, and lives are made new.

O Lord our God, make sensitive our spirits; grant wisdom to our minds and courage to our hearts to help lift the bonds that confine so many of thy children, our brothers. Amen.

37. The Carolers

And it shall come to pass afterward,
   that I will pour out my spirit on all flesh;
your sons and your daughters shall prophesy,
   your old men shall dream dreams,
   and your young men shall see visions.

(Joel 2:28)

A heavenly host, so sacred legend tells,
' Sang in the night to usher in the birth

145

Of One who came to be the Lord of life,
To bring good will to men and peace on earth.

One morning as I lay half-slumbering,
I heard sweet music sounding through the air;
It seemed the chanting of an angel host,
That sang of peace and brought glad tidings
*   there.*

No choir of heaven was this that came to sing
Beneath my window in the early morn;
It was the sound of maidens caroling
Who came to chant the news that Christ was
*   born.*

And if today the news be borne abroad
That Jesus came to earth to bring good will,
To end all strife, to make men dwell in love,
Not heavenly hosts, but youth, will bear it
*   still.*

These words might also have been included
as a Christmas poem, but I am placing them
here because of the last line. Even a hasty sur-
vey of our social situation would be inadequate
without a look at youth.

During nearly forty years of teaching in higher education—seventeen in two women's col-
leges and another twenty-two in two theological
seminaries—I have had many kinds of students.
They have been brilliant, dull, and in between;
from homes that were rich, poor, and again
mainly in between; from rural, urban, and suburban backgrounds; from many parts of the world.
146

A few—a very few—had to be asked to leave school because of some serious moral offense. Yet I cannot recall one who was mean, or nasty, or devoid of redeeming traits. Even the casualties could probably have been saved by wise understanding in conjunction with firmness.

Are today's students different? Yes, in some respects, but I believe not essentially so. The better academic preparation of the present student generation and a wider knowledge of the world through the mass media and other channels make them more mature in some ways. Yet many of them are emotionally more immature, for having grown up in a more permissive and a more affluent society, they have missed the discipline of both parental authority and economic hardship. As a result of these factors they submit to authority less readily than their predecessors, and conflict lies closer to the surface in asserting what they believe to be their rights. There is trouble on many campuses, and this seems to be an almost worldwide phenomenon.

I do not sanction all the turmoil that goes on today in the name of freedom, though I believe it is virtually always a small minority, not the main student body, that resorts to force and violence to try to get its way. Yet there is another aspect of the current scene which gives me great hope. This is that it is not only their own rights, but also the rights of the under-privileged and the oppressed, that they seek to

147

defend. In any list of the giant social evils of our time one would have to place war, racial discrimination, poverty, the placing of property above personhood, political tyranny, and the denial of basic human rights. Far more than their predecessors in less contentious days, and often far more than their elders whether in churches or outside of them, students today speak and act against such evils. In spite of excesses and errors, they move for the most part in the direction that should be—and through their action may well be—"the wave of the future."

So I do not despair of the youth of today. They will grow up, and I hope will not lose their zest for justice and sink into a middle-aged complacency. Most of them are sound at heart, and if our world is to come eventually to a time of "peace on earth, good will toward men," it is mainly the young who will lead the way.

We thank thee, God, for the young who see visions of a better world and will not be content with ancient evils. Give them wisdom with their zeal, and give us charity and understanding in our judgments. Amen.

38. Shall I Crucify?

So when Pilate saw that he was gaining nothing, but rather that a riot was beginning, he took water
148

and washed his hands before the crowd, saying, "I am innocent of this man's blood; see to it yourselves."

(Matt. 27:24)

Who crucified the Christ?
Judas for thirty coins
   His master sold,
As one today purloins
   A soul for gold.

Who crucified the Christ?
Who caused this mighty loss?
   Caiaphas prevailed,
And on a felon's cross
   Our Lord was nailed.

Who crucified the Christ?
Pilate washed his hands
   And let him die,
In soul like wind-blown sands,
   As you and I.

Who crucified the Christ?
The people had their way;
   They made him die.
He dies again today.
   Shall I crucify?

Personal responsibility is the crucial foundation of Christian ethics, of an ordered society, and of a just and peaceful world. Relatively few Christians or, for that matter, persons of good will who are not Christians, desire to hurt

149

anybody. What they do desire very often is to avoid a fuss, and especially a fuss that might implicate them personally. The wish not to become involved in a messy or demanding situation is a chronic frailty of human nature to which Christians are not immune. Yet by failure to act we inevitably become involved.

It is mainly because of this fact that the church needs renewal. This is why there is so much protest today against the institutional church as the defender of the *status quo,* indifferent to the cries of the poor, the downtrodden, and those of minority races denied their rights in a supposedly free society. Many of these protests overlook the amount of genuine concern over these matters that exists in the churches today. Yet there is enough basis for these charges to make all Christians need to engage in honest soul-searching. We *do* continue to crucify the living Christ.

Instead of further words of mine I wish to present parts of two quotations. Back in the 1930's I came across the poem of G. A. Studdert-Kennedy, "Indifference." It moved me deeply then, and it still does. Its theme is a comparison between what happened to Jesus at Calvary, "for those were crude and cruel days, and human flesh was cheap," and his return to Birmingham where "they never hurt a hair of Him, they only let Him die." The final stanza sums it up:

Still Jesus cried, "Forgive them, for they know
 not what they do,"
And still it rained the winter rain that drenched
 Him through and through;
The crowds went home and left the streets with-
 out a soul to see,
And Jesus crouched against a wall and cried for
 Calvary.[7]

To bring us nearer to the present, the following is from the message of the Fourth Assembly of the World Council of Churches in
Uppsala, Sweden, in July, 1968. It speaks
both from and to the churches.

We heard the cry of those who long for peace,
of the hungry and exploited who demand bread
and justice, of the victims of discrimination who
claim human dignity, and of the increasing millions who seek for the meaning of life.

God hears these cries and judges us. He also
speaks the liberating Word. We hear him say—
I go before you. Now that Christ carries away
your sinful past, the Spirit frees you to live for
others. Anticipate my Kingdom in joyful worship
and daring acts. The Lord says, "I make all things
new." [8]

So may it be in the world of tomorrow, if
Christians will cease to crucify Christ anew.

[7] From "Indifference" in *The Best of Studdert Kennedy*.
Copyright, 1924 by Harper & Brothers; renewed 1952
by Emily Studdert-Kennedy. Reprinted by permission of
Harper & Row, Publishers, and Hodder & Stoughton,
Ltd., London.
[8] *The Christian Century*, August 21, 1968, p. 1037.

Lord Christ, forgive us that we have sinned against thee by closing our hearts to the need of thy brothers and ours. Help us to carry thy cross and not to nail thee to it. Amen.

39. The Earth Thou Gavest

The earth is the Lord's and the fulness thereof,
    the world and those who dwell therein;
for he has founded it upon the seas,
    and established it upon the rivers.

(Ps. 24:1-2)

The earth thou gavest, Lord, is thine;
   We stand on hallowed ground.
In field and forest, mart and mine
   Thy handiwork is found.
O Lord of earth and sky and sea,
   In this our dwelling-place
We pledge to thee fidelity,
   Empowered by thy grace.

We would not claim what is not ours,
   Nor thy fair land despoil;
We hold in trust the golden hours
   Thou givest us for toil.
Our talents, too, of mind or hand
   Are ours by thy bequest;
To serve mankind in every land
   We strive at thy behest.

Beyond the turmoil of our day
  Whose tasks are scarce begun,
We long to hear the Master say,
  "Well done, thou faithful one!"
O save us, Lord, from selfish greed
  From pride of stubborn will,
As stewards both in word and deed
  Our calling to fulfill.

We would not yield to false acclaim
  Or bow in craven fear;
Above the proudest earthly name
  Thy Kingdom's goal shines clear.
O Lord of earth and sky and sea,
  In this our dwelling-place
We pledge to thee fidelity,
  Empowered by thy grace.[9]

One of the most constructive notes in the present concern for the renewal of the church is a broader conception of stewardship. Formerly its accepted meaning was the matter of making contributions to the church for its necessary expenses. Tithing has usually been emphasized, often without much regard for the fact that to give a tenth of one's income entails much more sacrifice on the part of the person living on the margin of subsistence than on one in the five-figure income bracket.

We ought to support the churches more gen-

[9] From "Ten New Stewardship Hymns," copyright 1961 by the Hymn Society of America. This and several of my other hymns have been selected for inclusion in such a brochure after a contest on an announced theme.

153

erously than most of us do, on the basis suggested by Paul to the Corinthian church, that each should give "as God hath prospered him" (KJV), or as the Phillips translation has it, "according to his financial ability" (I Cor. 16:2). But this is far from being all there is to stewardship. How one gains this prosperity is closely related to its larger meaning.

The belief that "the earth is the Lord's and the fulness thereof" should lead to stewardship of time, talents, labor, and all of one's possessions. Not all of these need be given to the church, but all should be put at God's disposal for the best possible use of them. There are many unglamorous tasks that must be done, but if one can see his daily work contributing even indirectly to human good, stewardship in the sense of a divine calling takes on deeper significance.

We have looked in the previous units of this section at some of the great problems of our time. Ramifying through all of them is the disparity between the economic resources, and hence the opportunities, of the "haves" and the "have nots," the privileged and the underprivileged peoples of the earth. Only as we move toward a better solution of this problem, both among the nations of the world and within our own, are the other problems likely to have any adequate or lasting solution. Let us try to give to God a good account of our stewardship of everything with which he has so bountifully blessed us.

Thou Lord of all the earth, all that we have is thine, and we hold it in trust from thee. Help us never to misuse or to waste thy gifts, but to use them as far as we are able in doing good to all men. Amen.

40. Forward!

I have set before you life and death, blessing and curse; therefore choose life, that you and your descendants may live, loving the Lord your God, obeying his voice, and cleaving to him.

(Deut. 30:19-20)

"To strive, to seek, to find, and not to yield!"
So sang the poet of a day long past,
A day we paint as time of peace, and shield
Our eyes from dismal shadows overcast.
But was it so? Men strove with brother man
And women grieved and could no comfort find;
The deep unrest that ever seems to span
The circling years then gripped our human
      kind.

Yet in that day the poet sang of quest,
Of walking forward, dauntless and secure;
By faith he saw the sun set in the west
And knew that after dark the dawn is sure.

155

*So in the strife and turmoil of our day
Faith beckons still and says, "Fear not the fray!"*

The poem with which we began this cycle of verses in quest of a better world was one of my earliest; this is one of the most recent. The only significance of this fact is that there is no time sequence in the need to press forward. The quotation from Tennyson's "Ulysses" comes from the nineteenth century but is equally relevant today. Still more time-transcending are the words attributed to Moses from the earliest days of our Hebrew-Christian faith. They take on special significance in this time of potential atomic destruction.

It would not be possible, were it desirable, to try to enumerate every kind of evil in today's world. Along with many good things for which to thank God, there are demonic elements in our society of which it may be said, as of the man from whom Jesus drove out the unclean spirits, that their name is legion. The man speaks in the first person, but both singular and plural, to say, "My name is Legion; for we are many" (Mark 5:9). So are our problems both individual and corporate. The facets of wrong that must be exorcised from our society are personal; they are individual both in the suffering of their victims and in the responsibility of those who cause them, more often by indifference than malice. Yet such evils are corporate,

156

magnified by society's close-knitness and re-
quiring a corporate attack by many persons of
sensitivity and courage.

The church has no panacea for such problems. Yet it does have leadership to give from
the moral insights of Christian faith. Christians
are citizens also, and together can do much to
change society. The mission of the church to
the personal spiritual life, vital though it is, is
not its only mission. Christians are called to
work with God with wisdom, energy, and faith
to make this a better world for humanity—all
segments of humanity—to live in.

This the church is doing, not sufficiently, but
more than its critics are wont to say. To illus-
trate, I have had some contact with the social action of The Methodist Church through several
General Conferences and while serving for nearly twenty years as a member, first of its Board of
World Peace and then of its Board of Social
and Economic Relations. These were thrilling
experiences which taught me watchfulness, lest
the other side prevail in an issue through lapses
in attention, but what is more important, that
it is possible to disagree deeply and still remain
friends. And little by little, the church moves
forward. As an individual my contribution was
small; as an arm of the church these boards
were helping to set the currents of thought in
a more Christian direction. I can see great
progress over the years in race relations and

other issues of the Methodist Social Creed, though there is still diversity of opinion in the church and plenty to engage us in forward movement.

It will not do for any of us to be weary in well-doing. "To strive, to seek, to find, and not to yield" is much-needed counsel, especially in times like these. God and the movements of history have brought us to a fateful day, potentially one of life or death, blessing or curse. Shall we not choose life?

Lord, help us to go forward, loving thee and all men, obeying thy call, cleaving to thee. Should our zeal flag, help us to remember that in thee is our strength, and in thy will and way is the healing of the world. Amen.

Variant Moods

41. Fruitage

I have seen the business that God has given to the sons of men to be busy with. He has made everything beautiful in its time; also he has put eternity into man's mind.

(Eccl. 3:10-11)

To view the sea of beauty, vast and fair,
And on its shores grow strong and keen of sight—
This is to see, in time, eternal light
And learn to know one beauty everywhere.

———•———

To answer that of God in every man
And over earth walk cheerfully,
This is to dwell, in time, within two worlds—
In Patmos and eternity.

———•———

"Pain is a passing thing, but beauty lives,"
So spoke a soul who, bound by body's chains,
Wrought valiantly. As dies the seed that gives
New life, pain passes but the fruit remains.

Within this section will be found some poems which do not fit readily into any of the preceding groups, poems which like the others

161

have come out of some aspect of my experience. On this page I am placing three quatrains which have quite different origins but enough of a common element to justify, I hope, their being grouped together.

For a good many years I taught philosophy as well as religion at Elmira College, and introducing my students to Plato was always a delight. The first poem is a paraphrase of some words in the *Symposium* (section 210). They stand just before the hauntingly beautiful ode to absolute beauty. Those familiar with this writing will recall that Diotima, a wise woman of Mantineia, is represented as discoursing with Socrates on the many forms of love, and she portrays the ascent of the soul upward, using earth's beauty as a stair, to "the true beauty— the divine beauty, pure, clear and unalloyed."

The second quatrain came out of a chapel address at the college by Rufus M. Jones, Quaker philosopher and mystic, in the best sense of that much-abused term. I suppose I have heard thousands of sermons in my life, some of them by very great preachers. Though they made their contribution at the time I heard them, I have to confess that I do not remember many of them very distinctly. This one I do. Rufus Jones spoke upon the Christian's "amphibian" existence, dwelling in two worlds at once. It was based on the word of the author of the book of Revelation: "I John, your brother, . . . was

162

on the island called Patmos on account of the word of God and the testimony of Jesus. I was in the Spirit on the Lord's day" (Rev. 1:9-10). George Fox's declaration that he desired to "walk cheerfully over the earth, answering that of God in every man" was also quoted. Perhaps the address impressed me the more because Rufus Jones seemed to me to exemplify so aptly his theme.

The third quatrain was written later, after I had injured my back and could not sit, stand, or lie down comfortably. It did not seem a serious injury, but as was suggested earlier, it was enough to disrupt my entire nervous system for a time. The friend who later became my housemate and who has shared my home and my life for many years brought to my attention the words of the artist Pierre Auguste Renoir when his arthritic hands made it difficult to paint. These words, to quote again from George Fox, "spoke to my condition."

As originally written, the poems were entitled "Birth in Beauty," "The Seer," and "Fruitage." I am here using the third as the title for the three, since in different ways they suggest the fruit that God stands ready to give in response to faith and an eager and persistent quest.

O God, the Author of all true beauty, we thank thee that thou hast made everything beautiful in its time and hast set eternity in the hearts of men.

163

Where this beauty has been marred by careless or evil acts, help us to heal the wounds, and help us each to add our small gifts to the making of a lovelier world. Amen.

42. *Accidie*

For affliction does not come from the dust,
   nor does trouble sprout from the ground;
but man is born to trouble
   as the sparks fly upward.

                 (Job 5:6-7)

When saints of old pursued the way to heaven
They walked with gruesome specters at their
   side—
Sloth, anger, envy, avarice, and pride,
With gluttony and lust—a deadly seven.

Drab sloth they feared, the sin of accidie,
(A good old word long buried with the saints)
A slackness, in the picture Chaucer paints—
The darkling gloom that halts activity.

This specter leered when men toiled over much
And saw no increment. It made them loath
To labor more, for heaviness and sloth
Shut out the light and held them in its clutch.

This "foul and lazy mist within the soul"
Is no dead demon sunk in Stygian slime.
He is alive, and stalks through every clime;
His clammy hand grips him who seeks a goal.

164

And now I feel his foul breath choking me—
I must arise and smite this accidie!

I have always tried to "walk cheerfully over
the earth," and think I have had a fair measure
of success, not with an exuberant *joie de vivre*
but a rather settled enjoyment of life. For this
I claim no credit, for I have been blest with
good health, useful work, and good friends to
sustain me. I have never had large salaries, but
enough for my needs. As for the sorrows, anxieties, and frustrations which have come to me,
as they do sooner or later to every adult, God
has helped me through them. This is why the
book is being written.

Nevertheless, I have had periods of feeling
bogged down, inefficient, unable to make much
headway either externally or in my own spiritual
life. These have not been limited to the period
of depression which led to the writing of *The
Dark Night of the Soul*. In retrospect I think
these feelings came most often when I under-
took too much and got too tired, but in any
case they came, unbidden and unwelcome. I
kept on working, but without glow or zest.

I have hesitated whether to include the poems
that came out of that state of mind, but have
decided to do so for several reasons. For one
thing, most of the earlier ones in this book have
reflected the beauty and goodness of God's
world, whether in nature, people, or our Chris-

tian heritage, but life has also a tragic and sordid side. It is still true, as in Job's day, that "man is born to trouble as the sparks fly upward." Furthermore, I believe that most persons, even the best of Christians, of whom I am not one, occasionally have such a sense of futility. Possibly the poems may do a little to point the way forward. Then, insofar as the book is autobiographical, they reflect a part of me that need not be hidden.

This "Accidie" [10] is a somewhat whimsical attempt to describe a serious matter of long standing in Christian history. It is an old English word which appears in Chaucer and in William Langland's *The Vision of Piers Plowman,* and Dante places its victims on the fourth ledge of purgatory. Its Latin form is *acedia,* one of the seven deadly sins and usually translated "sloth," though in the present usage sloth comes far short of expressing its depth of meaning. It is, I suppose, on the borderline of sin and illness—a sin if voluntarily yielded to, a sickness if one is unable to shake himself loose from it. In any case it is something to be rid of, by will power if possible, by corrective action where this is available, and in any circumstance by the love and the abounding grace of God.

We thank thee, loving Father, that thou art ever near—nearer than our own bodies which we would

[10] Pronounced ăk-sə-dē, as in *accident.*

yield to thee to be used as thou seest wise and good.
Help us to be rid of any barriers that stand between
us and our fullest living and thy fullest service.
Amen.

43. Wet Grass

If I say, "I will not mention him,
    or speak any more in his name,"
there is in my heart as it were a burning fire
    shut up in my bones,
and I am weary with holding it in,
    and I cannot.

(Jer. 20:9)

There is within me that which burns to speak,
But clogged with mortality is ofttimes choked.
Sometimes it bursts to utterance,
In words that warm me like a kindling flame,
Until, like fire upon wet grass, they die.
Then is the flame within me quenched,
Or smoldering, foul fumes corrupt my soul.

I wonder if God burns to speak to me
And finds his utterance fall on dew-drenched
    grass.
My soul! make haste to dry away the damp!
For if that torch, set burning on a hill,
Be choked in mist,
God's pity on himself and my cold heart.

The poem has a theme similar to that of
"Accidie," but in a different setting. Its con-

167

text is the eager yearning to proclaim a message which one believes to be God-given, yet with what appears to be complete futility in the attempt. I suspect that most preachers have felt this way at times. If one has not, it may be because he is a person of consummate skill in communication. Or, just possibly, because he is too insensitive to know or care much whether the message gets across.

In Jeremiah the "burning fire" was shut up in his bones because of opposition. The next verse speaks of whispering, terror, and cries of "Denounce him!" from familiar friends watching for his fall. In these days of mounting social tension, it is not unusual for something like that to happen to one who speaks out boldly for what he believes to be God's truth. But there is another and more common kind of "wet grass"—that in which one's words simply seem to make no impression, and one wonders whether the fault is in the people or in oneself.

In such a situation one is always tempted to blame others for the dullness of their response. This leads to a churlish and self-pitying feeling of not being appreciated, which in turn generates "wet grass" within one's own soul. Or one looks inward, as he ought to do, but emerges with an exaggerated sense of his own ineptitude and perhaps with a crippling sense of failure. In either direction futility stirs up "foul fumes" within the soul.

I shall not attempt to say here how to get out of this unhappy situation, though the next poems will venture some suggestions. But what of the latter half of this poem? And especially the last line? Is this not sheer anthropomorphism? And maybe blasphemous? I will not deny that its presupposition is that of a personal God, an understanding of God which need not be anthropomorphic unless God is reduced to our own human level. But I admit that the idea that God might pity himself is a bold figure, and quite out of place if God's self-pity were like ours in its nature and effects. I use it without apology because I believe in a suffering God who loves mankind enough to grieve both at his people's frustrations and at their lack of faith in his sustaining presence. The Kingdom comes so slowly—how much greater than yours or mine must be God's dismay! Yet I doubt he ever gives up hope.

Lord of my life, help me never to become fainthearted. Keep the fire burning in me until thy sun comes out and dries away the dew. In thee is my trust. Amen.

44. The Quest

O God, thou art my God, I seek thee,
my soul thirsts for thee;

my flesh faints for thee,
as in a dry and weary land where no water
is.

(Ps. 63:1)

If in the press of every day
The holy chalice slips sway;
If in the treadmill of my toil
My lamps are dry of festal oil;
If in the desert waste of things
I find no wells, no limpid springs:
Lord, touch with dew my parching
heart,
Anoint it ere it crack apart.

If in my own felicity
I walk as one who does not see;
If in a tangled underbrush
I move, and know not what I crush;
If in an avalanche of care
I use not mountain-moving prayer;
Grant me no highway to the Grail—
But light me, Lord, to find a trail.

I do not recall the circumstances under which
I wrote this poem. It was doubtless one of those
"dry times"—not a great cataclysm of soul but
a lapse in spiritual energy—which I believe
come now and then to most Christians. Somewhat paradoxically, either wet grass or a dry
and weary land will equally well describe it.

The devotional writers of an earlier day were
familiar with such dry spells and did not hesi-

tate to speak of them. In *The Imitation of Christ,* probably the most widely used devotional book ever written, other than the Bible, Thomas à Kempis gives his reader the sensible advice to "suffer patiently thine exile and dryness of soul till thou be visited anew and delivered from all anxieties." One is to wait patiently, but not supinely. In another passage he says graphically, "I shall alway put my mouth unto the hole of the heavenly pipe of that fountain so that I may at the least take a little drop to satisfy my thirst, so that I be not all dry; and though I may not be heavenly inflamed as the cherubim and seraphim yet will I enforce me to devotion."

There is a small but somewhat remarkable story connected with this poem. It was published in my *Holy Flame,* which came out in 1935. The book never had a wide circulation, and as the years passed, I was very busy with other matters and did not pay much attention either to the book or the poems in it.

After the end of the Second World War, when I was teaching at Garrett Biblical Institute (now Garrett Theological Seminary) in Evanston, Illinois, I was much surprised one morning to hear this poem in the Garrett chapel service. It was quoted by a man who had been a missionary in Malaysia, had been imprisoned in Singapore when the Japanese took the city, and then had been recently released with the

171

war's ending. His wife and children had lived in Evanston during this internment, and I greatly admired her faith and courage during the long period when she could not communicate or have news of him for many months.

But what of the poem? How did he come by it? As he told the story in chapel and has since supplemented it in conversation, he found it in one of the scanty bits of reading the prisoners were allowed to have. He memorized it, and he told us that he found it meaningful and helpful during those dreary days.

The story of the poem ends here, but not that of the man. He was later elected a bishop, and has long been an able and beloved leader of the church. The poem was in no way responsible for that, and I am sure that it was his own stalwart faith in God rather than a few words of mine that sustained him during his long imprisonment. But that these words should have gone somehow—there is no way of knowing how—to the other side of the earth, and into a prison, and so into the mind and heart of a prisoner, makes one realize the truth of William Cowper's familiar words:

> God moves in a mysterious way
> His wonders to perform;
> He plants His footsteps in the sea,
> And rides upon the storm.

Let the words of the poem and of this hymn
be our prayer today.

45. Rest in the Lord

For thus said the Lord God, the Holy One of Israel,
"In returning and rest you shall be saved;
in quietness and in trust shall be your strength."
(Isa. 30:15)

Sated with seeing, my sight grew blurred;
The vision splendid I did not see.
I rested, and looked, and in me stirred
The sense of God's reality.

———•·•———

I went apart to rest my soul one day,
To find the loam on which my life might grow,
And there I met thee, Lord, upon the way;
Thy radiant presence made my spirit glow.

The birdsongs in the trees were joyous lays;
In green and gold and silver camest thou near;
In quietness the silence sang thy praise;
In wordless tones thy voice spoke strong and clear.

To thee I rendered up my fretful care,
And let thee cleanse the dross within my heart.
For all thy suffering ones, Lord, hear my prayer;
Take thou my gifts and help me do my part.

In thee I rest and trust my soul to thee,
Thine is the Kingdom, Lord, and thine the victory.

173

To rest in the Lord is usually taken to mean spiritual quietness through trust of one's anxieties to God. This, of course, it does mean. But at least in a derivative sense, it means also to rest one's body, as to do one's work, in the Lord. This is the theme of this meditation.

Among the many wise sayings in *The Imitation of Christ* is this: "It is not done idly if thou perceive thyself ofttimes troubled or grievously tempted. Thou art a man and not God, thou art flesh and no angel." To apply these words to our own experience, the awareness that one is man and not God, flesh and not angel, can save one from excessive self-excoriation when the undesirable moods we have looked at—call them wet, dry, sluggish, heavy, or what you will—are upon us. They ought not to be encouraged, but neither should they be intensified by abnormal attention to them.

The earlier writers often saw this, but they had less discernment as to the relation of the state of one's body to spiritual health. Quite often as they misused or denied the needs of their bodies, instead of finding spiritual victory they fell into dark moods. However much they may have overworked their bodies in their zeal for the Lord, they appear certainly to have overprayed. Today we know that bodily health, and with it the rhythm of rest which is essential to effective labor, is an important asset to spiritual vigor. There is, of course, no exact correlation. We all know invalids and handicapped persons whose spiritual victory over the body puts us to shame. Yet in general the more rested and buoyant we are, the better our total encounter with life can be.

Like many other servants of the Lord, I had to learn this the hard way. When the pressure of duties and opportunities combined with spiritual pride in achievements to push a pain-wracked body almost to the point of a nervous breakdown, from which God graciously spared me, I learned then to say no to many demands. It was at about that time that I came across an illuminating word in Thomas R. Kelly's *A Testament of Devotion,* a word which could be dangerous if pushed too far. Speaking of the need to have a special concern for some things and an easy mind in the presence of desperately real needs which are not our direct responsibility, he says, "We cannot die on *every* cross, nor are we expected to."

So we need to rest in the Lord, spiritually and physically. This does not mean lethargy or complacency, God forbid. There is too much of that even in our harried society. But it means doing with vigor what we are called to do, taking time out to let God speak through the birds, the meadows, and the clouds, and leaving the results of our lessened labor in the hands of God.

Grant to us, God, keenness of sight to discern our calling. In thee we would labor and in thee rest, and in all things praise and bless thee. Amen.

46. *Hilltop at Morning*

If I take the wings of the morning
　　and dwell in the uttermost parts of the sea,
even there thy hand shall lead me,
　　and thy right hand shall hold me.
　　　　　　　　　　　　(Ps. 139:9)

I sat at morning on a friendly hill
And drank the poignant beauty of the day.
The sunlit clouds moved lazily and still,
A happy vale outstretched before me lay.
No solitary vigil this. New friends
Were with me in the silence of the morn
To catch the soul's upsurge that beauty lends
To questing minds—pulse quickened, life reborn.
The sky and earth were vocal, and yet mute:
The golden past poured out its harmony.
There Plato spoke of beauty absolute;
God's trombones blended in the symphony.
With voice of man and earth and sky so fair
It seemed that heaven's minstrelsy was there.

During the years when I was doing college teaching and for some time afterward, I had considerable contact with the Edward W. Hazen Foundation. This foundation then endeavored, among other enterprises, to nourish the religious life of students through various channels, mainly through the impact of Christian faculty members but also through books for student reading. My *Religious Living* was written by request as one of twelve in such a series of books, and surprisingly it stayed in print for thirty years.

A Hazen Conference provides the setting for this poem. Every year a group of faculty people, with some ministers and campus directors of student work, were brought together for a week of wonderful fellowship. There was always an invited lecturer of some note for intellectual stimulation, but it was also the meeting with old friends, the making of new ones, and the discussion of mutual concerns that made the Hazen Conferences so memorable. For several years I attended one at Lisle, New York, in a lovely rural setting which had unofficially been named Happy Valley.

Before commenting further, I had better admit that I do not ordinarily take well to early morning prayers. God seems to communicate with me much better after breakfast! Nor do I have a very favorable opinion of most "retreats" as I have experienced them. As conducted by churches, they are often in reality business sessions, which might as well have been conducted in the home surroundings at less expense and inconvenience, or they are

177

occasions for listening to a speaker who may or may not have something important to say. Sometimes in the "quiet times" there is an awkward and artificial silence when ordinary courtesy in not disturbing the meditations of others would be more effective. Yet there are exceptions to all these circumstances.

I recall most vividly this "hilltop at morning" experience. Those who wished to participate had been asked to bring along something— whatever we loved and wished to read—to share with others. As we sat together in the quiet of the morning, earth and air and sky, our heritage from the past and our challenges of the present, all seemed to blend in perfect harmony. What a gift from God is memory! As I sit at my typewriter now, I can see it all again and even hear the tones of some of the readers' voices. Some have died; some I have lost track of; some have remained my warm friends over the years. In recollection we are all back there together again.

One may call what occurred that morning a mystical experience, or simply a deeply moving awareness of the presence of God in a favorable environment. I do not object to calling it mysticism if, to quote Rufus Jones, we define mysticism as "a type of religion which puts the emphasis on immediate awareness of relation with God, direct and intimate consciousness of Divine Presence." I regret that mysticism has been so often understood as a negative withdrawal from the responsibilities of the earthly scene for what is assumed to be a union, rather than communion, with God. There have been mystics like that, but this was never the mainstream of authentic Christian mysticism, nor is it now.

Our God, we thank thee for memories that bless us, and for experiences that lift us up from the daily round into thy nearer presence. May our times of renewal stir us to more faithful service. Amen.

47. This Ministry

Of this gospel I was made a minister according to the gift of God's grace which was given me by the working of his power.

(Eph. 3:7)

Therefore seeing we have this ministry, as we have received mercy, we faint not.

(II Cor. 4:1 KJV)

We thank thee now, our God,
For years beneath thy sway,
For paths our fathers trod
To bring us to this day.
With vision high and hearts aflame
They wrought for thee in Jesus' name.

Thine ever-gracious hand
Hath led us to this hour.

179

> *Strong in thy strength we stand;*
> *Not ours, but thine, the power*
> *To view with faith the unborn years,*
> *For thou dost conquer craven fears.*
>
> *By love to conquer strife,*
> *To bring thy peace in pain,*
> *To heal a wounded life*
> *Is labor not in vain.*
> *We hold the chalice of thy love;*
> *Thy faithful servants may we prove.*
>
> *Take thou our lives, O Lord,*
> *We pledge to thee our all;*
> *In truth to preach thy Word,*
> *To serve thee at thy call.*
> *As thou didst speak through men of old,*
> *Lord, make our witness clear and bold.*[11]

This was written by request as the Centennial Hymn for the Pacific School of Religion, which observed its first hundred years of existence and service in 1966. It may be sung to the tune of "Arthur's Seat," if one wishes to try it.

For many years I have been rather closely associated with the ministry, and especially since 1940, when I began my seminary teaching at Garrett. It is a joy now to be able to encounter my former students at any major church gathering and in almost any part of the world.

I believe the Christian ministry to be the most

important vocation in the world, although this is not to say that everybody should enter it. I do not disparage the emphasis being given to the ministry of the laity—in fact, several years ago I wrote a book on this theme[12]—and when linked with stewardship in its broadest sense, it is a very important emphasis. Nor do I condemn one who, after the most careful and prayerful consideration, reaches the conclusion that his fullest service lies elsewhere than in the parish ministry. Yet the parish ministry is a work so vital that it ought not to be surrendered when its duties become arduous and the service seems not to be rewarded by the congregation's response. Without it, even such important ministries as those of counseling, civil rights, urban renewal, and the like would lose much of their spiritual as well as financial support.

One of the important developments of recent years is the opening up of the parish ministry, with full ordination and equality of status, to women. This has occurred in a number of major denominations, and others appear to be edging toward it. Official action does not remove social barriers, but these too seem to be melting somewhat. It is not to be expected that large numbers of ordained women will be serving local churches for years to come, for the pull

[12] *The Church and Its Laity* (Nashville: Abingdon Press, 1962).

of tradition is still strong; yet it is right that the opportunity should be open to those who are qualified and feel the call of God in this direction. I may have had something to do with the removal of the barriers to full Annual Conference membership in The Methodist Church in 1956, but the credit goes mainly to those able and dedicated women who were already serving in small charges as approved supply pastors.

So whatever our ministry may be, let us not grow faint-hearted in it! No gift of service that is offered in love and faith-filled devotion is lost in the eyes of God.

Lord of the church, I thank thee for the great heritage of thy servants in its ministry. Lord of my life, show me where best I can serve thee and let me not lose heart when the way is weary and the road is long. Amen.

48. *The Divine Patience*

All the ends of the earth shall remember
and turn to the Lord;
and all the families of the nations
shall worship before him.
For dominion belongs to the Lord,
and he rules over the nations.

(Ps. 22:27-28)

God strives.
Before the firmament was formed, the Eternal One
Envisaged all, and saw a battle to be won.
Through countless aeons of creative pain and toil
He shapes his world with everlasting moil.
God strives.

God feels.
The God who hears the gunfire of eternal war,
And smells the stench of sin, must suffer with
and for
Humanity. The God who heals with conquering
power
Must know himself the pangs of grief when shad-
ows lower.
God feels.

God waits.
Man lights a torch: in feverish haste he goes about
His task. He sees the light burn low: it flickers out.
The ever-striving, ever-suffering God relights
The torch, and labors on through agelong nights.
God waits.

It is not unusual for one whose life is committed to Christian service, whether in the ordained ministry or elsewhere, to become discouraged. Occasionally there are heartwarming evidences of progress in personal living or in an important social issue, but such moments are usually infrequent. Most of the time one must keep working away with the faith and the hope that in God's wider vision something good is being accomplished.

183

However, the poem is about God. Does he become discouraged? Certainly he must see a long delay in the coming of his kingdom. In the book of Revelation we find loud voices in heaven saying, "The kingdom of the world has become the kingdom of our Lord and of his Christ, and he shall reign for ever and ever" (11:15). This Hallelujah Chorus stirs us every time we hear Handel's *Messiah*, but the affirmation is proleptic, not past or present but a foregleam of the future.

The enormity of human suffering, arising not only from man's inhumanity to man but from what at times appears to be a capricious and purposeless universe, has given rise to the age-long problem of evil. To many minds it seems impossible to combine divine onmipotence with goodness. As a result God is thought to be non-existent, or an impersonal force of some kind (there are many variations on this theme), or if personal then finite. My honored professor, Edgar S. Brightman, believed God to be finite and ever struggling against "the Given" within his own nature, with limitation of power but not of goodness.

Since the poem may suggest a finite God, I hasten to disclaim it. I believe that God in infinite wisdom has limited himself by a mode of creation that precludes any quick and easy victory, but has not surrendered his ultimate control. Thus there is a continuing creation in which we are called to be God's servants and co-workers in fashioning an unfinished world nearer to his purposes. The greater part of human sin and suffering can be traced to man's misuse of his God-given freedom of choice and to a great network of social relations. The orderly processes of nature, if unharnessed, also may cause pain. Yet we would not wish to surrender, if we could, the great boons of responsible freedom, love and loyalty to one another, and the orderly world of cause and effect on which both scientific knowledge and much of our human happiness depend.

We are enjoined in the first chapter of Genesis to subdue the earth. In spite of all man's marvelous achievements, this has not yet been accomplished. The coming of God's kingdom and the doing of his will on earth, for which our Lord taught us to pray and by implication to labor, are long delayed. Must not God suffer at his human creatures' stubborn recalcitrance?

God of the long ages, God of eternity, we would do thy work more faithfully and in knowledge of thy patience would leave its results with thee. Amen.

185

49. The Maker

One thing have I asked of the Lord,
    that will I seek after;
that I may dwell in the house of the Lord
    all the days of my life,
to behold the beauty of the Lord,
    and to inquire in his temple.

(Ps. 27:4)

As poet strives to make his sonnet true
In form and meter, rhythm ringing clear,
And speak within its confines what his ear
Has caught of heaven's music, bring to view
His glimpse of deathless truth, and sing anew
Earth's melody for listening hearts to hear—
So does the Master Poet, God the Seer,
Strive to make clear what he would have men do.

He speaks his will in music, artist-wise;
His rhythm beats in nature's pulsing life;
His laws are forms that limit and make free.
Unchained, yet ever bound, his poems rise;
For he too makes, and sings in endless strife,
Struggling to mold the world that is to be.

Look in any dictionary which gives the derivation of English words, and you will discover
that the word poet comes from the Latin *poeta,*
which in turn is derived from the Greek
poietes as a noun and *poiein* as a verb, which
means "to make." Thus, by its derivation a poet
is a maker. I insert this brief excursion into

the etymology of words to suggest that the symbolism of this poem is not something I made up, but is embedded in the long history of language.

What is a poem? Opinions differ, but at least in the classical sense a poem must be an organic whole, yet with a structure and form in which each part relates to other parts and to the whole; it must possess beauty, though its kinds of beauty may be infinitely varied; and it must convey meaning. This meaning, at its best a universal meaning, comes from the mind and spirit of the poet and is designed to stir a response in the reader or hearer. These requirements are met perfectly in God and his relation to the world. God the Maker is the Poet of the universe.

Yet much depends on the reader's response. The poem may delight the senses, or intrigue the fancy, or quicken the thought, or stir deep and pure emotions in the recipient. Or it may do none of these things and fall on dry and barren ground. In that case, something is wrong either with the poem or its potential audience. The analogy of man's response to the words— or the Word—of God is clear. One *can* be dull to the greatest of all poems.

As was suggested in an earlier section, it is a pity that our Hebrew-Christian heritage has made so little of God as the divine Artist. The Bible has many terms by which to think

187

of him—Creator, Ruler, Judge, Redeemer, Father. All of these we need. And the Bible contains beautiful poetic passages which pay tribute both to the world of nature and to its Maker. Yet it lacks the final step of seeing artistic creativity as a basic note in God's own nature.

This poem gives some hints as to how the orderliness and beauty of the created world afford insights into the way in which we may conceive its Maker. They are hints only—no human mind can give a fully adequate explanation of why the world is as it is. It is a mystery our minds may properly wrestle with, but to fathom the whole mystery we should need to be as wise as God.

God's supreme disclosure is in Jesus Christ, and in him we find the life abundant, which is more important than an answer to all our questions. The church has contributed vastly not only to human good but to human understanding by making Christ the center of its message through twenty centuries. Yet he need not be our only approach to God. If we can find God in his world, why should we not trust the intuitions of the heart and see him as the Poet of the universe?

We thank thee, God, for manifold signs of thy presence in thy world. In thee we would live and be strong. Amen.

50. Transiency

The grass withers, the flower fades;
  but the word of our God will stand for ever.
                    (Isa. 40:8)

Some things
On wings
Of gossamer flit by
And then pass on to die—
Spring showers,
Bright flowers,
A rustling of the breeze,
A birdsong from the trees.

These stay
A day—
And then their quest is done,
Their pilgrimage is won.
On flow
The slow
Unstaying tides of time,
Naught lost that was sublime.

So I
Shall die:
The questing that was mine,
All in me that was fine
Forgot.
But not
In vain, I think, shall be
My passing melody.

When I began to prepare this collection I projected fifty as the maximum appropriate number of units. As I have gone along, I have selected from a considerably larger number of verses—many of them in lighter mood—those that seemed best to fit the mood of each major section. And as I come to the fiftieth, which shall be this last one?

The choice was narrowed to two. One of these was "Hope of the World," the hymn that received the award in a contest of the Hymn Society of America in 1954 for a new hymn in recognition of the Evanston Assembly of the World Council of Churches, whose main theme was "Jesus Christ, the Hope of the World." To discover that mine was given first place among about five hundred entries was one of my most spine-tingling experiences. Yet this has already found its way into a number of hymnals and need not be republished here.

So the choice is narrowed to a bit of verse that appears much lighter but deals with an agelong concern. This is the relation of being to becoming, of what is to what will be, of permanence to transiency. Heraclitus in the fifth century before Christ spoke words of wisdom that are still often quoted, "You cannot step twice into the same river, for other waters are continually flowing on." The Bible repeatedly emphasizes the transiency of human existence, and experience demonstrates it.

A generation ago, when belief in personal immortality began to be widely challenged, we heard much about the immortality of influence. As a substitute for the continuance of the individual self beyond death this is no immortality, for there is no guarantee that human life will continue to exist upon this planet—a fact more evident now than before the coming of the atomic age. As a promise that one will be remembered, if it is so understood, such pseudo-immortality applies only to the favored few. But as an affirmation that no human life, however brief or humble, terminates without some continuance of its "passing melody," it is a challenging and hope-inspiring thought.

Many people hesitate to think or to speak about death. This I believe to be a mistake. One should not be morbid about it, but the mature adult needs to think at least occasionally, not with dread and not with too great eagerness, of the time when his biological life will cease. Let us neither court death nor fear it. Our Christian faith gives adequate grounds for the assurance of eternal life by God's gift. These I have stated elsewhere and need not repeat. Though we cannot foreknow its nature with precision, we can know that in God's keeping all is well.

Paul, quoting matchless poetry from the Old

191

Testament which he knew so well and adding his own word, said it for us when he wrote:

But, as it is written,
> "What no eye has seen, nor ear heard,
> nor the heart of man conceived,
> what God has prepared for those who love him,"

God has revealed to us through the Spirit. For the Spirit searches everything, even the depths of God. (I Cor. 2:9-10)

So I believe. And so I conclude these observations on God's abounding grace.